Willie

Also by Teresa Nicholas

*Buryin' Daddy: Putting My Lebanese, Catholic,
Southern Baptist Childhood to Rest*

Willie

The Life of Willie Morris

Teresa Nicholas

UNIVERSITY PRESS OF MISSISSIPPI ♦ JACKSON

Publication of this book was made possible in part by a generous donation
by the Reba and Dave Williams Foundation for Literature and the Arts,
sponsors of the annual Willie Morris Award for Southern Fiction.

www.upress.state.ms.us

The University Press of Mississippi is a member of the Association of
American University Presses.

First printing 2016

∞

Library of Congress Cataloging-in-Publication Data

Nicholas, Teresa.
Willie : the life of Willie Morris / Teresa Nicholas.
pages cm
Includes bibliographical references and index.
ISBN 978-1-62846-105-3 (cloth : alk. paper) — ISBN 978-1-62846-106-0
(ebook) 1. Morris, Willie. 2. Authors, American—20th century—Biography.
3. Journalists—United States—Biography. 4. Editors—United States—
Biography. I. Title.
PS3563.O8745Z78 2016
813'.54—dc23
[B]
2015025342

British Library Cataloging-in-Publication Data available

And again, for Gerry

I had stories I wanted to tell. That's where the impulse comes from: your memory. Writing is memory, the burden of memory.

Willie Morris

Contents

Author's Note

⟨⟩

IN THE FALL OF 2012, ABOUT A YEAR AFTER THE PUBLICATION OF my first book, I received a call from my friend John Langston, who is the art director at the University Press of Mississippi. The press was considering publishing a biography of Willie Morris, he told me, and he proposed that I might be the person to write it.

I imagine that everyone who has ever published a book gets well-meaning suggestions from friends, readers, and relatives about what his or her next topic might be. These are rarely of interest, because in order to commit to the months of intense work involved in any project, a writer must feel a deep-down passion for the subject. John had an instinct that I would be hooked by a biography of Willie Morris, and he was right.

John and I had met Willie during the fall of 1969, when we were students at Yazoo High and he was the editor-in-chief of *Harper's*, come back to his native Yazoo City with his colleagues from the magazine to research an article about the pending integration of the public schools. Afterward I began to correspond with Willie—everybody, including students, called him by his first name. He was a great letter writer, prompt in his reply, warm in his response. He asked me to keep him up to date on what was going on in the recently integrated high school. Aware of my interest in journalism, he encouraged me to get a good liberal arts education, even writing me letters of recommendation for college.

Over the years we lost touch, but I read each of his books as soon as it came out. We reconnected in 1990, when he married JoAnne Prichard.

She had lived around the corner from my family in Yazoo City, and I had babysat occasionally for her boys, Gibson and Graham. Many years after meeting Willie, over dinner with JoAnne at the Steak House in Yazoo, he encouraged me to write my first book, peering at me over a plate of frogs' legs and asking, as I now know he asked of many aspiring writers, "Do you have a book in you?"

When I began researching this biography, I knew that I wanted to interview as many of Willie's friends as I could, especially from his childhood and college days. In the end, I spoke to more than fifty people who knew Willie, and though they are not all quoted directly in these pages, their voices can be heard in the tenor of the narrative. In my research I have also relied heavily on interviews with his family, and on the letters in the Willie Morris Collection at the J. D. Williams Library at the University of Mississippi.

JoAnne explained that Willie had a habit of tossing the letters he received into a cardboard box for posterity's sake. In 1995, he sold his collection of letters and literary memorabilia to the university. There are nearly fifty boxes of catalogued correspondence, as well as many dozens of boxes of clippings, magazines, manuscripts, contracts, financial records, speeches, programs, and that most elusive and captivating of all categories, ephemera. In addition, there are about thirty boxes that were delivered later to the university that are in the process of being catalogued, and I am thankful to the Morris family and to the library for allowing me to be among the first to sort through all of them.

It can be fascinating to read somebody else's mail, but it was especially fascinating to read Willie's. Most are letters to him, beginning in the 1960s when he started at *Harper's*, although there are a few that he wrote to his parents and maternal grandmother, Mamie, while he was studying at Oxford University. There are legions of letters from the fans of each of his books; love letters from girlfriends and wives; and letters from other writers, many of whom were his close friends—Eudora Welty, James Dickey, David Halberstam, William Styron, Winston Groom, among others. There are letters from presidents and letters from his publishers. There is also the occasional, poignant letter that he wrote to himself, and the occasional, playful note addressed "to my biographer." Then there are the oddities—in one box, an ashtray and a carefully preserved hairball from his beloved cat Spit McGee. In later years, when Willie had the help of a secretary, there are more of his own letters, drafts penned in longhand in black felt-tip before being typed. But that is not all. There are files about Willie's life at the B. S. Ricks Memorial Library in Yazoo City, and in Austin, Texas, copies of his college newspapers and the *Texas Observer* at the Dolph Briscoe Center for American History and the Perry-Castañeda Library. In short, a trove of material for a biographer.

The year after Willie's untimely death in 1999, he was voted by readers of the Jackson *Clarion-Ledger* as Mississippi's favorite nonfiction author of the millennium. Today, he remains a much-loved author and talked-about personality. Two previous accounts of Willie's life have been published: a scholarly bibliography/biography by Jack Bales, and a personal memoir/biography by Larry L. King. It is my hope that with the new details garnered from my many interviews and my library research, this accessible, illustrated biography will fill a void in the literature for the general reader.

Teresa Nicholas
Jackson, Mississippi

Willie

ONE

Growing Up "on the Edge of the Delta"

Then it was a lazy town, stretched out on its hills and its flat streets in a
summer sun, a lethargic dreamy place, green and lush all year except for
those four stark months at the end and the beginning, heavy with leafy
smells, at night full of rumblings and lost ghosts. . . .
—*Willie Morris,* North Toward Home

IT WAS AN OLD TOWN, FOR THESE PARTS. IT HAD ITS BEGIN-
nings in the 1820s, as a landing called Hanan's Bluff, at the point where
the Yazoo River, in its snaking southwesterly trajectory toward the
Mississippi, touched a line of loess hills, making it the only service-
able port for 180 miles. When the developing town was incorporated
in 1829, it would be called Manchester, after the city in the northwest
of England that was the hub of that country's cotton industry.

Mississippi's Manchester was laid out purposefully: Main Street
spanned four north-south blocks, its foot tucked neatly into a bend
of the river, and other principal streets were named for presidents
Washington, Monroe, Madison, and Jefferson. Soon a bank opened,
along with several hotels; warehouses sprang up, and the shoreline
was handsomely bricked. Splendid homes, built from the easy supply
of local lumber, began to take shape on the side streets. Then, in 1839,
the town picked a new name for itself, one to reflect the river's growing prominence in its everyday life: Yazoo City.

The city grew partly on the hills and partly on that great expanse
of flat land, the Mississippi Delta. This wasn't a true delta, formed at
a river's mouth, but a floodplain that opened in a great yawn over the

Baby Willie.

state's northwest corner. This ancient land was bound on the west by the Mississippi River and on the east by its rowdy tributary the Yazoo. The Delta stretched from present-day Vicksburg to Memphis, in a profusion of forests and canebrakes, crossed with muddy creeks and bayous and harboring a welter of insects and birds, reptiles and other animals, including bears, deer, and panthers.

For centuries, this land had been the hunting grounds of Native Americans, but in a series of treaties between about 1800 and 1830, the Choctaws had ceded it to Mississippi. Eventually the flat land would be drained and cleared and, with its unrivaled fecundity, would become inextricably linked to the growing of cotton. By 1840, Yazoo County was prosperous, exporting twenty-five thousand bales yearly, and the city had become a vibrant port, where smokestacked riverboats loaded cotton bound for Vicksburg, New Orleans, and beyond, and on returning carried amusements and culture back to the fledgling town. At the end of the decade, Yazoo City was named the county seat.

By the Civil War, Yazoo County's population had grown to over twenty thousand, with slaves outnumbering whites about three to one. Especially after the fall of Vicksburg, in 1863, the county saw its share of fighting. There were thirteen skirmishes in or around the city, which was occupied by Union forces on six occasions. A makeshift Confederate naval yard was set up about a half-mile from downtown, where a rough ironclad, the CSS *Arkansas*, was concocted from scrap metal and salvaged engines, and managed briefly to menace the Union fleet headquartered near Vicksburg. In March 1864, fierce fighting erupted on Yazoo's Main Street, leaving thirty-one northerners and six southerners dead. Two months later, the elegant Greek Revival courthouse was burned.

After years of tumult, of war and Reconstruction, Yazoo City, "like Topsy, was just growing up," according to an early-twentieth-century newspaper article (alluding to the character in Harriet Beecher Stowe's *Uncle Tom's Cabin*). Then, on a windy day in May 1904, more than two hundred buildings burned, encompassing an area twelve blocks long and three blocks wide. The fire was said to have started when a boy playing with matches ignited the home of John Wise, between Main and Mound streets. When the *New York Times* reported on the fire, they described Yazoo City as "the wealthiest town in the Mississippi delta," and cited 2 million dollars' worth of damage. "The only buildings of consequence directly exposed to the holocaust which escaped were the Court House and the Fannie J. Ricks Memorial Library," the article stated, "and through some queer prank of fate both of these were unharmed, although surrounded by fire on all sides." Within a year, Main Street had been rebuilt with rows of two-story brick storefronts. But in 1927, Yazoo City met another disaster when the levees near Greenville, Mississippi, broke and inundated the Delta. Floodwaters stood hip-deep, and didn't recede for weeks; there was no electric power for more than a month.

By 1930, fifty-five hundred people lived in Yazoo City. In a local history book, *Yazoo: Its Legends and Legacies*, the times are described as "two-fisted," with men routinely carrying pistols and with gunfire sounding in the streets, although this may not have been so different from other small towns in the region. During the spring of 1930, three shootings occurred in Yazoo, with the most infamous taking place on Main Street, when the mayor shot a doctor and the editor of the newspaper before killing himself.

It was this spirited place that Henry Rae Morris and Marion Harper Weaks Morris discovered when they arrived in Yazoo City during the Depression, with their infant son. William Weaks Morris had been born on Thanksgiving Day, November 29, 1934, in Jackson, but the following year the family moved to Yazoo City after Rae accepted a job there. Willie would later write that his mother, a graduate of Jackson's Methodist-run Millsaps College, who had also studied in Chicago at the American Conservatory of Music, cried about having to move to this rough outpost, some forty miles from the capital city.

To his mother's chagrin, Willie wrote, the people there "still talked about the Great Flood of 1927, that catastrophic breaking out of the Mississippi," when "the waters, muddy and infested with snakes, had inundated the houses on the street where we were to live." But Yazooans didn't relive their memories of just the Great Flood. They mulled the outcome of the Civil War and speculated about the location of the sunken Yankee gunboat, the USS *Cairo*, in the Yazoo River. They retold the heroic story of Casey Jones and the wreck of the Cannonball Express in 1900 at nearby Vaughn. And they perpetuated a tale about the Great Fire of 1904, which attributed the conflagration to a witch who lay buried in Glenwood Cemetery beneath a heavy chain—minus the one link through which she had escaped to take her revenge. Theirs was a place brimming with history, and a place that made legend out of history.

In the lyrical opening paragraph of his first book, his memoir *North Toward Home*, Willie described what a visitor would likely see upon coming to his adopted town:

> Half an hour north of Jackson on U.S. 49, not far beyond the Big Black River, the casual rolling land gives way to a succession of tall, lush hills, one after another for twelve or fifteen miles. In spring and summer the trees and underbrush are of an almost tropical density, and the whole terrain is grown over with a prolific green creeping vine, right up to the highway, and sometimes onto the concrete itself when the highway workers have let up a day too long. On a quiet day after a spring rain this stretch of earth seems prehistoric—damp, cool, inaccessible, the moss hanging from the giant old trees—and if you ignore the occasional diesel, churning up one of these hills on its way to Greenwood or Clarksdale or Memphis, you may feel you are in one of those sudden magic places of America, known mainly to the local people and merely taken for granted, never written about, not even on any of the tourist maps. To my knowledge this area of abrupt hills and deep descents does not have a name, but if you drive up and down them once on a fine day and never see them again, you will find them hard to forget.

Willie Morris found the "abrupt hills and deep descents" impossible to forget. In time, both the place and its inhabitants, along with their history and legends, would come to haunt his writing.

✦ ✦ ✦

Yazoo was a small southern town, with small-town leanings befitting the times. In those days, religion meant fundamentalism buoyed

by revivals, with regular travel to the little
sister churches out in the county for all-day
preaching and singing and "dinner on the
ground." Racial segregation was strictly up-
held, and not much questioned, at least by
the white townspeople. Yazoo was a farm-
ing community, and the citizenry stayed
close to the land, in tune with the passing of
the seasons and the vagaries of the weather.
They had an abiding sense of their own past,
and ample pride in it. The place was terribly
isolated then, reachable by two-lane gravel
roads. People stuck together, helped one another, and in the cool of the evening—there,
it always seemed to be summer—they sat
out on their front porches, saluting one another with friendly greetings, entertaining
one another with stories.

Marion Morris. After graduating
from Millsaps College in Jackson,
she studied at Chicago's American
Conservatory of Music.

In Yazoo City, Rae became the agent for
the Cities Service Company. At his head-
quarters located along the railroad tracks beyond Fifteenth Street,
there were two slim storage tanks and a small office building. From
this base, Rae traveled the county delivering diesel fuel and gasoline
to filling stations, farms, and gins. In a very early childhood memory,
Willie recalled his father's workplace:

> My father had a huge green truck—so large I had to sit on a box to
> see out its windows—and from there came the heady smell of Cities
> Service gasoline. There was a gas station to play in, and somewhere
> down a wide street and beyond a railroad track a place with tanks,
> platforms to jump from, a cool warehouse with dirt for a floor, and
> room for the dogs to run and bark in the tall grass on a hill.

Later Rae Morris would take another job, for the Goyer Company,
a wholesale supplier of foodstuffs to small groceries and plantation
stores; Goyer had a large warehouse in Yazoo's downtown, where he
worked as a bookkeeper. Marion Morris taught piano, and played the
organ at the First Methodist Church.

Henry Rae Morris in a baseball team picture taken in Camden, Tennessee.
He is third from the right in the back row.

Rae Morris had grown up in Camden, Tennessee, in the low hills west of Nashville, the son of William L. and Nancy Stigall Morris. Rae's father, who was known as Will, had studied law and was a successful businessman who served in the Tennessee legislature, but Willie described his own father as "*country*, in the way that he was tuned to its rhythms and its cycle; he and his Tennessee people were simple, trustworthy, straightforward, and good as grass." After graduating from high school, Rae joined the army to serve in World War I, but before he could ship off to Europe, the armistice was declared. He found his way to Jackson, Mississippi, where he took a job with the Standard Oil Company. There he met Marion Harper Weaks, and they married in May 1929. Willie was to be their only child.

Rae was a thin, taciturn man, taut in the way he held himself, but he relaxed with a few favorite pastimes. One of these was baseball, the game that had given him his nickname, "Hooks," for the agile way he could execute a hook slide. Rae was also a contract bridge enthusiast who took pleasure in playing dominoes with the firemen at the stationhouses, discussing baseball with the Lebanese immigrants in their stores on West Broadway, and spending quiet hours in the woods or in a rowboat on one of the muddy lakes outside town. As for church, Rae Morris attended only once a year, on Easter, and if the preacher happened to call at his house, Rae would likely take *True Detective* or *Field and Stream* to the weeds out back and thumb the magazine's pages until the preacher had departed.

When they first arrived in Yazoo City, the Morrises lived in the second block of Grand Avenue, a wide thoroughfare in the newer, flatter section of town, lined with gracious homes. They rented part of a white frame house from an elderly, well-placed lady, Letitia King, affectionately known as "Aunt Tish." When Willie was barely a year old, he contracted scarlet fever and suffered convulsions. None of the white doctors could be found to pay a house call, so the black physician, Dr. L. T. Miller, was summoned to attend the toddler. This incident, as later retold to Willie by his maternal grandmother, Mamie, would provide him with an early sense of the South's pervasive racial issues, which would become a central theme in his writing. In *North Toward Home*, he says that he asked his grandmother which door the doctor had used, and goes on to characterize the South of his youth:

> The child Dr. Miller saved, having come in to him through the back door, was a child born into certain traditions. The South was one, the old, impoverished, whipped-down South; the Lord Almighty was another—anthropomorphic and quick-tempered, a natty beard on his Anglo-Saxon face; the Negro doctor coming around back was another; the printed word; the spoken word; and all these more or less involved with doom and lost causes, and close to the Lord's earth.

In 1938, the family bought a modest Cape Cod–style house four blocks farther north on Grand Avenue, taking a mortgage of $3,800. The Morris property was narrow but deep, almost half an acre, with the backyard abutting one of Yazoo's many alleyways, which in turn bordered the meager houses of the black families who lived on Calhoun Avenue.

Willie in his stroller on Grand Avenue, near the house his family rented.

The Cape Cod house the Morris family bought in 1938. Willie lived there until he left for college.

Mrs. Morris's Steinway baby grand took up most of the home's front room, along with a few of her prized antiques—carved chairs with needlepoint cushions sewn by her mother, and an heirloom spinning wheel. On the wall hung a framed photograph of Willie. In *North Toward Home*, he wrote of long late afternoons spent in his bedroom listening to the sounds of children practicing their scales and sonatas, and then hearing his mother rendering the piece "like Mr. Mozart would want it played." She taught Willie piano, too, until he was nine, when he resisted the six-day-a-week regimen. He reported that his mother "grew intemperate," but that his father, who usually kept out of things, told her, "Let him alone to grow."

Marion Morris was as loquacious as her Tennessee husband was taciturn, and she and her mother, Marion "Mamie" Harper Weaks, instilled in Willie an abiding interest in their family history. His distant forebears had been the Harpers of Virginia, founders of Harpers Ferry, who later settled in frontier Mississippi. Willie often wrote about them and their prominent roles in the twentieth state: about his great-great-great-uncle Cowles Mead, an acting territorial governor, and another great-great-uncle by marriage, Henry S. Foote, whom Willie called "my true family hero." Editor of the prominent newspaper the *Mississippian*, a U.S. senator, and governor of Mississippi, Foote was "a fighter for the Union, an uncompromising enemy of the Southern extremists" in the years before the Civil War. Still, when the war came, he accepted a seat in the Confederate Congress.

George W. Harper of Raymond, Mississippi, Willie's great-grandfather, provided him with one of his treasured family stories. Harper was founder and editor of the *Hinds County Gazette*, and in 1863 Union General William Tecumseh Sherman reportedly ordered the newspaper's presses thrown into the town well. In addition to being a journalist, Harper was a major in the Confederate army, a member of the state legislature, and mayor of Raymond. He also fathered sixteen children, including Willie's grandmother, Mamie, the young-est, born in 1878. About Mamie, Willie wrote: "She, of course, was the one who was the repository of those valiant tales and vanished troubles, who made that old time come alive for me."

During the summers when Willie was a boy, he would board the Greyhound bus in Yazoo City to visit his mother's relatives in their brick house on North Jefferson Street in Jackson's leafy Belhaven neighborhood—in addition to Mamie, there were his grandfather Edmund Percy Weaks and his maternal great-aunts Mag and Sue Harper. Percy worked in a potato chip factory at the corner of Farish and Griffith streets, and "every afternoon at four he would come home smelling of potatoes, and fetch from his satchel two bags of chips, crisp and hot from the oven." Sometimes Willie accompanied Percy to the factory. "We munched on potato chips all day, from nine to four," Willie wrote, "and came home so full of salt and potato grease that we had to have five or six glasses of ice water apiece at supper."

Percy had been born shortly after the Civil War, in 1869, the same year as Willie's great-aunt Sue; Mag had been born just before them, in 1866. To Willie, theirs was "a different world filled with Yankees, poverty, and death, and the dreadful passing of time," yet he loved visiting them. In the family's garage, Percy constructed model steam-boats for him and regaled him with tales about boat races on the Mississippi River. They scaled fig trees, swam at Livingston Lake, and banged on toy drums; it seemed there was nothing Percy wouldn't do. It was from his grandfather that Willie inherited his sense of fun and love of pranks.

They also attended baseball games, "the ultimate joy of my child-hood summers," Willie wrote. They would walk to the state fair-grounds to watch the Senators, a Class B team in the Southeastern League. Beginning when Willie was about three, his father taught him the rules of the game, during outings to Yazoo's Goose Egg Park. In that wide, grassy loop on Grand Avenue, Rae would rough out a diamond with cardboard bases and practice hitting with Willie. Later, when Willie was older, "almost every summer afternoon when the heat was not unbearable," they would go to the baseball field, where his favored childhood dog, Skip, would chase the straggling fly balls.

Rae would also take Willie into the woods that ringed Yazoo City and show him how to find his way using natural markers such as a split tree or a mangled limb. He took him cane-pole fishing, too, at Wolf or Five Mile Lake, where, if they were feeling lazy, they might rent a small boat and simply drift, pulling in perch, bream, and goggle-eye for a fry-up at home. "Ours was a nonverbal relation: we never talked about anything 'important,'" Willie wrote. Yet from Rae, he learned to love the silent woods and the still lakes, the crack of the bat, and the company of a good dog.

When he was four years old, Willie started Sunday school at the First Methodist Church, while his mother played hymns at the service. "My Negro nurse would bring me at nine-thirty in the morning, and wait out back with the other nurses while our teachers told us stories about the Bible, or helped us make religious posters, or led us in singing," he wrote. Here he met other members of the Methodist cradle roll, Edwin "Honest Ed" Upton, Kay King, Marion "Peewee" Baskin, Margaret "Pep" Pepper, Wilson "Henjie" Henick, and Nancy Jo Golden.

On weekdays, many of these same children would meet up again. It was the custom that youngsters would take an afternoon nap, staying out of the intense heat, in the hope that this would protect them from contracting polio. But after the children were bathed and dressed in starched and ironed clothes, their nurses would escort them to the playground at the Main Street School. This stern-looking building, with its high windows and soaring Ionic columns, had been under construction during the time of Yazoo City's 1904 fire. The schoolhouse was located on a large triangular plot, next to the classically beautiful B. S. Ricks Memorial Library, the oldest library building in the state.

Willie with his nurse in front of his family's home on Grand Avenue.

To reach the school, those children who lived on the southern end of Grand Avenue, including Willie, would walk along Canal Street, with its turbid run-off waters from high in the hills, teeming with crawdads. While their nurses fanned and chatted, the preschoolers jostled over the swings and cavorted at the base of the Confederate Monument, which had been erected in 1909 by the United Daughters of the Confederacy with its lofty inscription, "As at Thermopylae, the greater glory was to the vanquished."

In 1939, Willie started kindergarten at St. Clara's Academy. Not long after the Civil War, the Sisters of Charity of Nazareth had founded the school, which offered the only kindergarten in Yazoo. The Sisters, with their flowing black habits and white

Willie in Glenwood Cemetery, which would figure prominently in his writing.

bonnets, sat the children at tables of four, where they taught them the alphabet and popular songs such as "Billy Boy," "Sailing, Sailing," and Stephen Foster's "Oh! Susanna." The Sisters also gave instruction in the Catholic faith, but during these lessons the majority of students, who were Protestant, were left on their own with their coloring sheets. In kindergarten, Willie met Hilary "Buba" Barrier, who would become his best friend, along with Doyle "Moosie" Moorhead, Vanjon Ward, and Ralph Atkinson. Ralph lived across the street from St. Clara's, and every day at recess his mother would bring him a glass of fresh milk.

At the Methodist Sunday school and at St. Clara's kindergarten, Willie got to know the classmates that he would matriculate with to elementary school and study with all the way through high school. They would become his circle of closest friends, those with whom he would perpetrate pranks and hijinks, those with whom he would come of age. Together they would generate the many indelible memories that Willie would conjure into stories throughout his writing life.

TWO

School Days in Yazoo

"A Pleasant, Driftless Life"

———————◆◆———————

Yazoo, Yazoo, in closing let us say, that forever and a day,
we'll be thinking of you, Yazoo, Yazoo.
—*Yazoo City High School Alma Mater*

"WHEN I WAS FIVE MY MOTHER TOOK ME BY THE HAND INTO
the two-story brick school on Main Street and left me in the care of
Miss Bass, a stern old lady who looked as if she would bite." And so
William Weaks Morris entered first grade, in Public School Number
One (Number Two being the school that black children attended
in those segregated years). Willie described the interior as "all long,
shadowy corridors, smelling faintly of wax and urisol." At the end of
his first day, when his nurse neglected to pick him up, he and Buba
Barrier held hands and walked the seven blocks home together.

Myrtle Bass was the principal and Willie's first-grade teacher. The
students from St. Clara's kindergarten were assigned to her class,
which met for only a half-day; pupils who hadn't been to kindergarten and didn't yet know their ABCs stayed the full day, as did those
who lived out of town and so had to take the school bus. In the classroom and on the playground, Willie saw that Main Street School
was made up of town and country, flat lander and hill dweller, the
daughters of plantation owners and the sons of sharecroppers. It was
here that he first became aware of class differences among his own
race.

From the start of Willie's scholastic career, Marion Morris pushed
him to be popular and to make all A's. And although she praised her

son in front of others, in private she could be hypercritical. Jimmie Ball, a childhood friend who lived cattycorner from the Morrises on Grand Avenue, remembers, "She stayed on him, motivated him." For the most part, Willie excelled in elementary school. His class-mate Margaret Pepper (later Grantham) recalls that in kindergarten, when Sister Francis Edwin had asked if there was anyone she wanted to sit next to, she'd volunteered, "William Morris." Now she again sat behind Willie, since their last names fell in alphabetical order. One day in spelling practice, the students were given the word *rhythm* to parse. When Pep whispered to Willie that she had trouble with it, he explained, "Oh, I remember it by the first letter of each word in the sentence 'Ralph Has Your Tie, Hillbilly Morris.'"

But in fourth grade, when Willie's teacher, whom he referred to as "Miss Abbott" in *North Toward Home*, misstated the capital of Missouri as St. Louis, he made the mistake of correcting her and felt that he'd created an adversary. Then he threw a spitball at Kay King and for six weeks had to stay after class to figure interminable long divisions. On his next report card, he managed only a "C" in arithme-tic. He later wrote: "I was nine, and for the first time my grades were

Willie (left) as the bridegroom in a Tom Thumb Wedding, with Ralph Atkinson (center) as the minister and Vanjon Ward as the best man. Inspired by the marriage of P. T. Barnum celebrity Charles Stratton (stage name, Tom Thumb) to Lavinia Warren, such mock weddings were popular, often as a way to raise money for charity.

Willie with Huntz Hall during the actor's visit to Yazoo City. In the 1950s, performers came to town to promote their films.

erratic and my conduct report questionable. My own mother, who had pushed me onward as the nicest and brightest boy in the county, predicted I would never work out." But even during that troublesome year, school had its rewards: "There were trips in the late afternoon to the town library, a cool and private place, where I would sit in a quiet corner and read the latest serials in *Boys' Life* or *Open Road for Boys*, or examine the long rows of books and wonder what was in them and why they were there."

During Willie's early school years, World War II was declared, altering the tenor of life in Yazoo City. Mothers volunteered for the Red Cross, families grew victory gardens, citizens of all ages sold war bonds and collected scrap metal, and Yazoo's children went on the lookout for "spies." The war consumed Willie and pushed that other war, between North and South, into the distant past. He kept a diary of the major battles, which he read about in the *Memphis Commercial Appeal* and the *Jackson Daily News*. When his next-door neighbor, Bob Edwards, sent him a German helmet from the front, Willie took it to school for show-and-tell. At the cavernous Dixie Theater, at the intersection of Broadway and Main, Willie and his friends haunted the Saturday Kiddie Matinee, where you could spend the entire day watching war movies for ten cents, although if you volunteered to sing patriotic songs during the talent hour, you got in the following week for free.

At last old enough to be released from the custody of their nurses, Willie and his gang ripped and ran around the town, up and down the narrow alleyways, hiding from the Germans or playing kick the can, returning to their homes only when the streetlights flickered on. Willie was fun, cute with a cherubic face, always looking for something to do, and often that something was a little mischievous. A natural leader, he was usually the one who spurred on his friends. This is how he described their high spirits:

> There was something in the very atmosphere of a small town in the Deep South, something spooked-up and romantic, which did extravagant things to the imagination of its bright and resourceful boys. It had something to do with long and heavy afternoons with nothing doing, with rich slow evenings when the crickets and the frogs scratched their legs and made delta music, with plain boredom, perhaps with an inherited tradition of contriving elaborate plots or one-shot practical jokes. I believe this hidden influence, which will explain much that follows, had something to do with the Southern sense of fancy; when one grew up in a place where more specific exercises in intellection—like reading books—were not accepted, one had to work his imagination out on *something*, and the less austere, the better. This quality would stay with one, in only slightly less exaggerated forms, even as a grown man.

They baked oatmeal cookies, adding to the traditional recipe doses of "castor-oil, milk of magnesia, and worm medicine for dogs," and left them for the Wednesday meeting of the Women's Society of Christian Service. Although Mississippi prohibited the sale of alcohol, they managed to send a case of bourbon to the Tuesday meeting of the ladies of the First Baptist Church. Around Yazoo, on occasion, a dead rat might turn up in a mailbox. Other ornately wrapped, inappropriate gifts were bestowed on unsuspecting residents, including "six-month-old moonpies, live crawfish, grubworms, and hot bacon grease." All these mischiefs would later find their way into Willie's books.

When Willie was in the third grade, his great-aunt Sue died. During the funeral, he later wrote, "I stood in front of the open coffin and looked down at her for a long time, even when no one was in the room. . . . I said to myself, I have to memorize what she looks like so I won't forget her." He was given a puppy "as a kind of consolation prize against death," an English smooth-haired fox terrier with a pointy nose, which his father had shipped from a kennel in Missouri. "I was an only child," Willie wrote, "and he now was an only dog."

He named him Skipper, "for the lively way he walked." Mostly he called him Skip, but he also called him, at various times, Old Skip and Boy. In the opening pages of the diary that Willie started around this time, he filled in the line "In case of accident or serious illness, please notify_____" with the name "Skipper J. Doggiefellow." In an entry the young diarist wrote, "Skip is smart. Skip is *very* smart." Later he added, "Skip is still smart."

And he was. Skip grew to be an extraordinary dog, and an eager participant in Willie's practical jokes. They became a twosome. Across-the-street neighbor Jimmie Ball says he can still see Willie bounding down the steps of the Morrises' house hollering, "Squirrel, Skip!" and the dog scampering up the inclined trunk of a tree in the front yard. Willie trained Skip to play sports. "I cut the lace on a football," he wrote, "and taught Skip how to carry it in his mouth, and how to hold it so he could avoid fumbles when he was tackled." The sight of the wily terrier running with the pigskin prompted many a car on Grand Avenue to stop so the driver could exclaim, "Look at that dog playin' football!" Skip was independent-minded, too. He traipsed around town by himself and ran errands for his master. Willie would attach a little leather pouch to Skip's collar, place a quarter inside, and tell Skip to run to Goodloe's Grocery, located a few blocks away near the railroad tracks, and buy himself some bologna. Bozo, who sliced the sandwich meats at Goodloe's, was in on the joke, of course.

Although they weren't yet old enough to drive, Willie and Buba Barrier got into the habit of taking Buba's family's sedan through Brickyard Hill and other black neighborhoods, "anywhere that white adults were not likely to spot us." Sometimes Willie borrowed his family's DeSoto, and this led to one of Skip's most famous exploits. Margaret Pepper Grantham describes how Willie would stretch out on the front seat with his hands on the bottom of the steering wheel, while Skip occupied the driver's seat, with his paws on the wheel's upper curve. One or two of Willie's friends would be in the back seat, so it would look as if Skip were chauffeuring them. They'd also be giving Willie instructions about which way to turn and when to put on the brakes. He had a device called an "ultra-mike," which he'd purchased for two dollars from a mail-order catalogue, that could project the user's voice from any radio, making it sound as if it were coming over the air. Pep recalls that Willie would broadcast to bystanders, as if Skip were talking, "Hey look at me, I'm driving this car!"

Willie with his dog Skip. Willie is in costume for a high school spoof.

And then there was baseball. In those days, Yazoo City was crazy for the sport, and so was Willie. The field was situated near the county fairgrounds, close to the grassy strip known as the "airport." On lingering spring and summer days families would congregate on the wooden bleachers, shelling roasted peanuts and urging on their favored boys. As for the players, they might become seasonal heroes, or face the ignominy of mediocrity or defeat.

"Like Mark Twain and his comrades growing up a century before in another village on the other side of the Mississippi, my friends and I had but one sustaining ambition in the 1940s," Willie would write. "Theirs in Hannibal was to be steamboatmen, ours in Yazoo was to be major-league baseball players." Willie played both high school and American Legion junior baseball and was on that team in 1950, the year they won the Mississippi State Championship. The players, he recalled, were given "shiny blue jackets, with 'Miss. State Champions' written on the back; I was so happy with that jacket I almost wore it out." When he grew too old for American Legion baseball, for a season Willie joined a semipro team, the "Screaming Eagles," competing against college and high school players from around Mississippi.

Baseball was so popular in Yazoo City that the local radio station, WAZF, sponsored a call-in trivia contest, awarding a dollar and a

Willie (back row, second from left) with the semipro baseball team the Yazoo Eagles.

pack of razor blades to the daily winner. Willie collected the jackpot so many times, remembers Jimmie Ball, "they finally quit the program, because he was the only one winning." But baseball in Yazoo wasn't only about local teams and contests. On any summer weekend afternoon, many of the men would have radios at hand, hanging on the broadcasts of the big-league teams. Willie explained, "Even among the adults, baseball was all-meaning; it was the link with the outside."

In the late 1940s and early '50s many of those radios were tuned to Gordon McLendon—a.k.a. the Old Scotchman—who announced for the Liberty Broadcasting System. One day, while Willie was listening to a game and tinkering with his father's short-wave radio, he stumbled on something of great import: the Scotchman's broadcasts were delayed, and more than that, they were re-created with descriptive details and studio sound effects. He recognized this discovery as "a weapon of unimaginable dimensions," which ignited his artistic imagination. "Instead of being disappointed in the Scotchman, I was all the more pleased by his genius, for he made pristine facts more actual than actuality, a valuable lesson when the day finally came that I started reading literature." Willie realized that he could use the short-wave broadcasts to amaze the local fans—Bozo and the guys gathered at Goodloe's, for example, and the firemen at the stationhouses—by making prescient play-by-play predictions. For his power to foretell hits and runs, he became known as "the Phantom," graced with "extra-vision." But the scam proved short-lived, when his father found him out and unveiled his secret.

For many generations, Glenwood Cemetery had been a beloved place of Yazoo City's young people, a storehouse of history and a site of great beauty, a microcosm of the town itself with both flat land and hills, thick with old cedars, magnolias, and live oaks. And there was the irresistible pull of certain graves—the large plot said to belong to eight hundred Confederates who had perished in the apocryphal Battle of Benton Road; the supposed tombs of John Hancock's two grandsons, who allegedly died while passing through the Delta; and the chained resting place of the witch of Yazoo. On Halloween, Willie and the other children would visit the witch's grave in the company of an adult, and from there walk to Main Street, where they would be treated to ice cream at Carr's Drug Store.

It was in this cemetery that Willie perpetrated one of his best-known pranks. He told a younger boy, Jon Abner Reeves, that he would give him a quarter if he would rattle the chains on the witch's grave. And so one June evening, Willie and Ellis "Strawberry" Alias stationed themselves near the haunted spot, while Jimmie Ball and others waited with Jon Abner at the cemetery gates. When the sun finally set, Jon Abner set out alone up the narrow path. As he approached, Jimmie recalls, "Willie blew his horn and Strawberry held up a sheet over a tombstone. At that time, the road was gravel and you could hear Jon Abner running, shouting, 'There's a ghost in there!'"

But Willie's childhood pranks weren't all innocent fun. On occasion, by his own admission, he acted toward black children in a way that was cruel. When he was twelve, he set on a boy of three who was merely walking along the sidewalk. He writes that he "slapped him across the face, kicked him with my knee, and with a shove sent him sprawling on the concrete." Willie felt a "secret shame," later reflecting on relations between the races:

For my whole conduct with Negroes as I was growing up in the 1940s was a relationship of great contrasts. On the one hand there was a kind of unconscious affection, touched with a sense of excitement and sometimes pity. On the other hand there were sudden emotional eruptions—of disdain and utter cruelty. My own alternating affections and cruelties were inexplicable to me, but the main thing is that they were largely *assumed* and only rarely questioned.

In time, Willie's attitude about race would be influenced by his father's and grandmother Mamie's moderate views. Rae often commented about black citizens, "If they pay taxes they oughta get to vote. It's as simple as that." Willie would eventually become a passionate advocate of civil rights, but it was a journey that would begin after he had left for college.

◆ ◆ ◆

Then in the fall of 1948, Willie entered Yazoo City High School. The building was located at the end of Grand Avenue, at Canal and College streets. Above the entryway towered a statue of the Greek philosopher Plato, and under it the promise *Education/ Knowledge*; nearby stood a massive stone tablet carved with the Ten Commandments.

Three years after the end of World War II, automobiles were still in short supply, and Willie and his classmates often walked to school, or they caught a ride with their fathers on the way to work. At lunchtime, some ate in the cafeteria, but many went home; afterward, the students congregated on the low wall near College Street, or if the weather was pretty, sat in little groups on the grass, chatting in anticipation of the bell. Willie described the times this way: "For going to a small-town high school in the lower South in the early 1950s was a pleasant, driftless life; we dwelled on philosophical problems like 'school spirit' and being 'popular,' and we expected a 'good time' as if it were owing to us."

Willie's priorities, as set down at an early age by his mother, had been to get good grades and be popular, and now she exhorted him to join in as many extracurricular activities as possible. His friends shared these same goals, and so they applied themselves to their academics, tried out for the sports teams, played instruments in the marching band, ran for class offices, and enrolled in clubs. Says Margaret Pepper Grantham about the class of 1952: "We were above average, we were goody-goodies, and teachers liked us."

Willie excelled at Yazoo High, studying history, algebra, biology, chemistry, Spanish, and Latin. For three years, he had English with Omie Parker. She was a dedicated educator with a devotion to the classics, and her classes were demanding, with plenty of assigned homework, including reading Chaucer and Shakespeare. As a teacher, Willie wrote, she was "despairing of mediocrity, and incorruptible, and perhaps for all these reasons, scorned and misunderstood." He continued:

Omie Parker, Willie's high school mentor, whom he called "the best writing teacher in my life."

> But as for me, I had a long, painful way to go before the things she tried to teach me could take hold. I read her books and parsed her sentences to stay on her good side and to get A's. The books themselves meant little to me, and made almost no impression at all on the way I lived or how I saw experience. I memorized the rules of the language, but my own prose style was like a Mack truck churning up mud. I did not understand my own intelligence, and even if I had I would not have known what to do with it.

Willie and his friends behaved like "good old boys," especially when it came to downplaying their intellect. He explained, "So you would banter about grades as if they were of no account, curse the teachers, and develop a pose of indifference to ambition in all its forms. And you would speak the grammar of dirt-farmers and Negroes, using *aint's* and reckless verb forms with such a natural instinct that the right ones would have sounded high-blown and phony."

During his senior year, Willie performed with the marching band; his instrument was the cornet, similar to the trumpet. He was also the sports editor on the yearbook, the *Mingo Chito*, and played baseball and basketball. That year, the basketball team finished with a 7-6 record. As for baseball, the team made its worst showing since 1946, winning only one game, but according to the yearbook, "Left fielder

Harold Kelly, who coached Willie in high school basketball and baseball. He remembers Willie as a dedicated athlete.

Willie Morris captured team batting leadership and the traditional trophy with an even .300 clip." He led the team in stolen bases and sacrifices. His coach Harold Kelly remembers that Willie was fast, but that he wasn't so much a born talent as he was a dedicated player, "a good student of the game."

But Willie's real pride lay in writing for the high school newspaper, the *Flashlight*. As sponsor of the paper, Mrs. Parker recognized Willie's talent early on. When he was a freshman, he was already contributing editorials, including one in which he endorsed the States' Rights Democratic ("Dixiecrat") Party and praised the "Mississippi Way of Life," a euphemism for segregation. By sophomore year, he had his own column for the *Flashlight*, "The Sports Closet," which appeared alongside his photo. Junior year he was the paper's coeditor, and in his last year editor-in-chief. "My *Flashlight* prose resounded to strange, esoteric rhythms, supplemented with ambitious, unheard-of words," he wrote. But the year Willie edited the paper, it received awards from the National Scholastic Press Association and the Columbia Scholastic Press Association.

Willie played cornet in the Yazoo High band. From left to right were Ralph Atkinson, Willie (here holding a trumpet), Wilson Henick, and Vanjon Ward.

Willie (seventh from left) with his high school basketball team. His best friend, Buba Barrier, is immediately behind him.

The *Flashlight* wasn't Willie's only early foray into journalism. At the age of twelve, the year that his father gave him his first typewriter, a secondhand Smith-Corona, he was already writing about sports for the *Yazoo Herald*—although in his first article, reporting on a Yazoo High School baseball game, he forgot to include the final score. He also broadcast sporting events for WAZF, whose slogan was "1230 on your dial, with studios high above the Taylor and Roberts Feed and Seed Store, in downtown Yazoo City, the Gateway to the Delta." He emceed his own music program, "Darkness on the Delta," named for the theme song of popular Yazoo-born orchestra leader Herbie Holmes. The show was call-in format, and if he didn't happen to get any requests on a given night, he would make up his own playlist. Once when he broadcast all classical music, he received a phone call threatening, "Play some Tennessee Ernie . . . or we're gonna come down there and tear that place up." He changed the selection.

Because Willie played the cornet, the Yazoo City post of the American Legion asked him to sound "Taps" at military funerals for Korean War soldiers. Along with Ralph Atkinson and Henjie

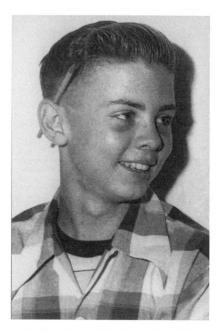

For his column "The Sports Closet" in the *Flashlight*, Willie's signature photo showed him with a pencil behind his right ear, a pose he would adopt again.

Henick, he alternated playing the melody at the gravesite and, from a distant stance, the echo. They "played for more funerals than we could keep count of," Willie said, and he got to know the Legionnaires and their war stories. And so as an adolescent, he had a haunting experience that would come to have a lasting effect on his writing, inspiring the novel *Taps*, which he would work on for much of his adult life. At the funerals, he preferred the part of the echo, where a wobble on the high-F wouldn't be so noticeable. But more than that, as he would write in *Taps*: "An echo, I would learn, was a kind of life in perpetuity, remote and immune, distant lingering notes from afar, sweetly voyeuristic."

Although Willie was busy at school, he and his friends, both boys and girls, also led an active social life. On the weekends, they often went to Pepper Camp, the vacation house of Margaret Pepper and her family, located outside of town at Five Mile Lake. Pep's folks always chaperoned, with her dad cooking up hamburgers or his popular spaghetti sauce. During the day they swam, boated, and fished, and in the evenings, they practiced dance steps, such as the jitterbug. These were fun times, and rarely serious, but Pep remembers that once she sat down on the sofa next to Willie, and he confided to her his future ambitions. Willie's voice was never loud, and when he wanted to make a point, it would get even softer. On that occasion, Pep says, he told her that "he wanted to write the truth." He was referring to how the Japanese people had been portrayed during the war, and after. "This made me think, at the time, that maybe we don't always hear the truth," she recalls, "and that Willie realized it before any of the rest of us had given it a thought."

Later on in high school, when the teenagers began dating, they spent less time at Pepper Camp. Willie started going out with Dee Phillips, a pretty blond majorette two years younger than he was.

They might attend the midnight show at the Dixie Theater or go to the dances held after football games, or ride north into the Delta to hear the popular Vicksburg-based group the Red Tops perform their eclectic brand of jazz and blues.

The friends had been together from elementary school, some from the Methodist Church cradle roll, and as graduation approached, they vied for votes—for Mr. and Miss Yazoo High, Most Handsome and Most Beautiful, Friendliest Girl and Boy, and other honorifics. According to the list next to Willie's quarter-page photograph in the 1952 yearbook, he was elected Most Versatile Boy, Wittiest Boy, and Senior Boy Most Likely to Succeed. He was also a member of the National Honor Society, the Student Council, the National Athletic Scholarship Society, and Quill and Scroll (an honorary society of high school journalists), among others. Along with Buba Barrier, he was co-vice president of the senior class. Buba was voted Most Handsome.

As Willie's classmates made their plans for college, most to attend in-state schools, he struggled with a decision. Like his best friend, Buba, he was thinking of going to the University of Mississippi. Afterward, he dreamed about returning to marry his girl, the majorette, and managing her family's plantation. But Willie's father had other ideas. Rae Morris traveled a thousand miles round trip to visit the University of Texas in Austin, which he had heard was "the best and certainly the biggest state university in the South." He returned to Yazoo City with high praise for the institution—for its grand buildings, for its baseball field "dug right out of stone," and for its student publication, the prize-winning *Daily Texan*. He urged

Willie, with the Smith-Corona typewriter his father had given him, in the family dining room.

Willie's senior portrait in the Yazoo High yearbook, the *Mingo Chito*.

Willie to apply. And so even as the seniors attended casual socials and formal dances, wiener roasts and hayrides, Willie wrote, "Something different was stirring around in my future, and I would brood over the place where I was and some place where I would end up, and for days I carried a map of the University of Texas in my shirt pocket."

Finally, it was graduation night, May 28, 1952. In the school's gymnasium, the president of Jackson's Belhaven College addressed the fifty-five graduates, and the class of '52 presented the school with a gift of two drinking fountains. The ceremony, which had begun with the school's sixty-piece concert band playing the "Overture Militaire," ended with the seniors singing the alma mater, "Yazoo," music for which had been written only a few years earlier by band director Stanley C. Beers.

The next day, William Weaks Morris published his final editorial in the *Flashlight*. No longer did his prose sound like "a Mack truck churning up mud," but already presaged his adult writing style:

> The crowd had departed, and one dim light remained in the building. As I approached the exit, the words of the speaker once more came back to me, "carry out the faith your school has shown in you." I hesitated on the brink of the threshold, gazing at the hall I knew so well, and I seemed to be part of the place. I fully realized then—perhaps for the first time in my life—that I'd been going to school all these years for a purpose, and that all the work, the fun, and even the worry and hardship were directed toward one end—helping me get along in life.
>
> I walked into the night, away from the building. I looked back but the old place was all closed and dark, and I turned and made my way from one life into another.

In his long solitary visits to Glenwood Cemetery, Willie had made a decision. He would leave Mississippi and head west to Texas.

THREE

"Ready to Lick This Old World"

The University of Texas

It took me years to understand that words are often as important as experience, because words make experience last, but here, in the spring of my freshman year, there were men who were teaching me these things.
—*Willie Morris*, North Toward Home

"ONE COLD, DARK MORNING" WHEN WILLIE WAS SEVENTEEN
years old, he boarded a Southern Trailways bus in Vicksburg,
Mississippi. As he traveled over the Vicksburg Bridge and through
east Louisiana, with its flat fields of cotton, he was reminded of the
Mississippi Delta. A little farther along the highway, he passed the
turnoff for the small town of Bastrop, where his grandfather Percy
had been born. In Monroe, around 7 A.M., the bus stopped for breakfast; after that, the land became hillier and woodsier. Several hours
later, in Shreveport, Willie stretched his legs, ate lunch, and changed
buses. Shortly after noon, the new bus left, and not long afterward,
entered east Texas.

Two dozen stops later, after a fifteen-hour journey, Willie finally arrived at the Austin bus terminal, on the corner of 10th and
Congress streets. Leaving the station, he saw before him the Texas
state capitol. The great domed building, constructed in the late
nineteenth century of limestone and red Texas granite, soared over
downtown. Texans liked to point out that if you counted to the top
of the star in the Goddess of Liberty's hand, their capitol was 14.64
feet taller than the one in Washington, D.C.

Willie standing in front of the iconic Tower at the University of Texas.

The only other building of any appreciable height in the Austin skyline was the Tower at the University of Texas. Finished in 1937, fifteen years before Willie arrived, the classically inspired Tower provided the focal point for the campus. Its French-educated architect, Paul Philippe Cret, had designed eighteen other university buildings, many in a Spanish style replete with red tiled roofs. By the early 1950s, the University of Texas had grown beyond its original forty acres and boasted more than twelve thousand students. The population of the university and town combined was fourteen times larger than that of Yazoo City.

Wearing unfashionable green trousers and displaying his National Honor Society fob on his watch chain, Willie "emerged from that bus frightened and tired." Delta Tau Delta had been alerted that he was a good prospect for their fraternity, and several members met him at about nine o'clock. They were surprised at how young he looked—"like a child," Wayne Agnew remembers. After shaking hands, Willie said, "I'm hungry. Let's get a hamburger." That evening, driving around campus with the Delts, he had to agree with his father about the university's impressive facilities. He spent that night in the fraternity house.

The new freshman set about selecting his classes. First semester, he enrolled in Spanish, music, English, and one journalism class, Radio Workshop. During Willie's four years at the university, he would follow this pattern, studying mostly the liberal arts, but also mixing in many courses from the Journalism Department. In high school he and his classmates had participated avidly in extracurricular activities, and in the 1950s, university students were no less enthusiastic joiners. The young men, dressed in sports shirts and pleated slacks, and coeds, in their circle skirts, loafers, and bobby socks, signed up for clubs and committees, sports teams and fraternal organizations. "I myself shared that compulsion to join," Willie wrote, "and join I did."

By the end of September, he had pledged Delta Tau Delta, known for its scholars, student government leaders, and athletes. He played trumpet in the ROTC band and took part in student government, including a committee that recommended increasing the campus minimum wage to seventy-five cents an hour. As for sports, he found time to play on intramural teams. But most important, Willie began writing for the student paper. Although he had flirted with becoming a baseball play-by-play announcer, by the end of freshman year he would commit himself to print journalism.

Willie on campus, in a yearbook photo. One student remembers him looking "like a child."

The widely admired *Daily Texan* had first published in the fall of 1900, as a weekly, but by 1913 it had become a daily, with the masthead claiming it to be "The First College Daily in the South." In the nineteen teens, the forward-thinking paper had begun subscribing to a wire service and reporting on state and national events. Starting in 1935, the *Daily Texan* even owned its own typesetting machines and printing press. At times throughout the newspaper's history, its editors had come up against university officials, battling over vital issues such as censorship. The office of editor was regarded as a key position on campus, elected by the student body.

During Willie's freshman year, the *Daily Texan* moved into a new, state-of-the-art journalism building in the heart of the campus. It was massive, built on a slight hill and entered by an expansive concrete stairway. Willie described it this way: "Its physical set-up was impressive; there were individual offices for the important editors, a 'city room' with a big copy desk and two wire-service tickers, and a chute to drop the copy down to a modern composing room below. I felt good just walking into those offices, for it was obvious they were designed for professionals."

Willie in a characteristic pose, as writer for the *Daily Texan*. He assumed the editorship in 1955.

Ambitious, talented, and armed with a letter of reference from his high school English teacher, Omie Parker, Willie wasted no time in writing his first article, which appeared on September 17, under the headline "Well, Here I Am: Stiff Upper Lip Helps Freshman Survive Test." In the piece, he reminisced about Yazoo City, "just an average, everyday American town with people you could look up to and respect." He admitted to feeling homesick and to being "awed by the smallness of myself." But he also expressed confidence that someday soon he would become part of this big, new place. He concluded with a brash self-challenge: "I have made my way from one life into another, and now I am ready to lick this old world."

He got down to licking it. The *Texan* editor awarded Willie his own column, an uncommon honor for a freshman. His assignment was to scour scores of college papers from around the country and synthesize the news from their campuses. One day after his debut article appeared, his first "Neighboring News" column was published. Like many of the two dozen pieces he would write that semester, it was lighthearted and laced with puns; again Willie introduced himself to his readers, and again he invoked his hometown, calling it "a wonderful place . . . home of the most beautiful girls, the friendliest people, and the most intelligent dogs in Mississippi." During the next four years, he would often bring stories to the *Daily Texan* from his hometown and state.

But there was also a serious side to the column. "Here I began to read about strange ideas like integration, and issues of academic freedom," he later wrote. He had access to newspapers from campuses as diverse as Millsaps College in Jackson, Mississippi, Stanford University, Oklahoma City University, and the University of Pennsylvania. "I gradually began to see the differences in all these papers; the ones from Harvard or Yale and a few big state universities were almost daringly outspoken, and kept talking about 'conformity' and 'self-satisfaction' in a way that both mystified and aroused me." Willie's exposure to these "strange ideas" would help him to mature as a college journalist.

In his spring semester, he survived the hazing of "hell week" exacted of all fraternity pledges. He signed up for classes in speech, geology, English, and math and was inducted into Phi Eta Sigma, a freshman honor society for men. That semester, he also took on three new tasks for the newspaper: reporting on intramural athletics and contributing to two columns about university life, "Campus Sidelights" and "Assignment Forty Acres." In his first "Sidelights" column, titled "Brackenridge 'Refugees' Not Thirsty These Days," he comically described the havoc wreaked by a broken water pipe in his dormitory. For three years, he would live in Brackenridge Hall, a mottled yellow-brick building with a cornerstone from 1932. From his fourth-floor window, he could see the intramural playing fields below.

Willie could have lived with his fraternity brothers in the Delta Tau Delta house, which was air-conditioned (a rare luxury for the time). But he chose not to, and although he did attend the obligatory Monday night dinners, he didn't visit often. For one thing, the fraternity house was removed from the center of campus; for another, the boys, who hailed mostly from large cities such as Dallas and Houston, would haze him by insisting he do pushups or eat "square" meals, in which the movements of the knife and fork had to trace right angles. By comparison, life was secure and familiar in

Brackenridge dorm, where the residents were more like the country boys he had known in Yazoo City.

In *North Toward Home*, Willie said he relished "the mad, rudimentary life of the dormitory" and its occupants—especially the mischief-making third-floor baseball players "from small ranch towns and middle-sized cities on the plains." Brackenridge, he wrote, was one of the things "that made my lonely and superficially gregarious freshman year tolerable, and helped shape my knowledge of that campus." By his own admission, he "became a sort of poet laureate of that group, the resident egghead, it may have been, because I at least tried to study my books."

Mississippi-born Frank Lyell became one of Willie's most influential professors. Lyell, who had studied at Millsaps College, the University of Virginia, and Columbia University, had received a Ph.D. from Princeton; he was a book reviewer for the *New York Times* and a friend to a wide circle of southern writers, including Allen Tate, Katherine Anne Porter, and Eudora Welty. Lyell taught freshman English, and once assigned his students the task of writing their autobiography. For his paper, Willie wrote: "My dog Skip and I wandered the woods and swamplands of our Mississippi home shooting rabbits and squirrels," prompting the esteemed professor to ask, "Who was the better shot, you or the dog?" But in Lyell's classroom the lessons that Omie Parker had begun to instill in Willie finally took hold. Under Lyell, he was inducted into a world of ideas, into understanding "the power not merely of language, but the whole unfamiliar world of experience and evocation which language served. That world was new, and the recognition of its existence was slow, uncertain, and immature. Books and literature, I was beginning to see, were not for getting a grade, not for the utilitarian purpose of being considered a nice and versatile boy, not just for casual pleasure, but subversive as Socrates and expressions of man's soul."

Also that seminal first year, Willie was invited to the home of two married graduate students, where he encountered "more books than I had ever seen before in a private dwelling—books everywhere and on everything." The sight was so strange that he wondered if the books might be for sale or if they were on exhibition. "It is a rare experience for certain young people to see great quantities of books in a private habitat for the first time, and to hear ideas talked about seriously in the off hours," he wrote. When his hostess asked Willie what he planned to do after graduation, he announced, to his own surprise, "Be a writer." Afterward he vowed to go the library, "to read every important book that had ever been written," though he had no idea where to begin.

> But once this fire is lit, to consume and to know, it can burn on and on. I kept going back to the library, taking out tall stacks of books and reading them in a great undigested fury: Hemingway, Faulkner, Wolfe, Dreiser, anything in the American literature and American history shelves that looked promising. I started buying Modern Library books with the money I made writing for the newspaper, and I pledged to myself, as Marilyn Monroe had, that I would read them all, and in alphabetical order.

Several years later, when Willie finally did move out of Brackenridge Hall, first into the Delta Tau Delta fraternity house and then into a shared apartment, Jack Little, one of his roommates, recalls that Willie "brought all of his books, and they lined every wall of the room." Another roommate, Henry Jacoby, remembers that Willie would often hand him a book, saying, "Hankman, why don't you read this? I think you'll like it." The University of Texas had succeeded in awakening Willie to "the acceptance of ideas themselves as something worth living by."

+ + +

In 1953, two presidents were inaugurated—in January, Dwight D. Eisenhower for the United States, and in October, silver-haired, movie-star-handsome Logan Wilson for the University of Texas. Despite the ongoing "red scare" and fear of nuclear war, the decade of the fifties proved a mostly quiet time on college campuses. The university, headed by Logan and the Board of Regents—the latter appointed by Governor Allan Shivers—was deeply conservative. In two years' time, Willie would find his ideals pitted against theirs.

But now, in his sophomore year, he signed up for, among other classes, American literature, chemistry, economics, News Gathering and Reporting, and Beginning Typewriting, to hone the keyboard skills required of a reporter. Although Willie had taken typing at

Logan Wilson, president of the university from 1953 to 1960.

Yazoo High, which was obligatory for both boys and girls, he still typed with two fingers, as he would all his life. On the *Daily Texan* masthead, he was at various times listed as assistant sports editor, night reporter, and night sports editor. As of September 23, he began penning a new column, "The Round-Up," which he would write until he graduated. The weekly column dealt with college life—profiling professors, taking jabs at campus issues such as the lack of parking spaces and the student activity fee—and was mostly upbeat. But at times Willie took a serious, even philosophical tone, waxing poetic about "the Flow of Life and Time" on campus or interviewing students about the top five historical figures they would most like to meet.

In May 1954, as his sophomore year was coming to a close, Willie profiled Ronnie Dugger, who had served as editor of the *Daily Texan* and, after graduation in 1951, had matriculated to England's Oxford University. While he'd been editor, Dugger had instilled "some impalpable force into the campus," Willie wrote, "a force that caused people to stop and read and think." In Willie's "Round-Up" column, there now seemed to be a new sense of urgency to his prose, and he touched on issues, such as conformity and censorship, that would soon preoccupy him. Dugger became his role model. At the end of that semester, Willie was inducted into two more honorary societies—Goodfellows, which recognized student leaders, and Silver Spurs, which was charged with caring for Bevo, the longhorn steer who was the university's mascot.

The next year, Willie's third, he took classes in psychology, literature, economics, math, and several more in journalism—News Editing, Advanced Reporting and Ethics, Press and Contemporary Affairs, and Editorial Writing. He stepped up his work for the *Daily Texan*, with his name appearing on the masthead as assistant sports editor and day editor; second semester, he became sports editor, but still found time to write editorials, news stories, and his "Round-Up"

column. From the fall of 1954 through the summer of 1955 he contributed some 120 articles.

Willie had been a schoolboy prankster, and while at the University
of Texas he was still fun loving and mischievous. According to a history of the *Daily Texan*, there was a tradition of practical jokes at the
paper, and the "sportswriters were often at the heart of the pranks."
During football season, Willie, along with fellow Silver Spurs Dan
Burck and Dean Smith, decided to transport the fifteen-hundred-
pound Bevo V twelve hundred miles to the University of Notre
Dame, outside South Bend, Indiana. Not only would they haul the
longhorn to the football game against the Fighting Irish, but along
the way Willie would dispatch articles to the *Daily Texan*.

The escapade began with the trio hitching their trailer to a
'53 Pontiac equipped with new tires for the journey. Leaving on a
Wednesday, Bevo's caretakers planned to drive north to St. Louis,
then on to Chicago, arriving Saturday morning in South Bend.
Things did not go precisely as anticipated. "Every five hours or so
it becomes urgent to take Bevo out of his trailer for a walk," Willie
wrote. And whenever they stopped en route, they found themselves
explaining to the locals that Bevo was "not a milk cow who had
sprouted horns." Not surprisingly, the strange caravan had problems
finding places to lodge. One night they bunked free of charge in a
motel called the Longhorn. The manager had consented to put them
up because the boys promised to tie Bevo in front of the motel, providing some complimentary advertising. On the gridiron, Texas was
routed, but Willie got three stories out of the jaunt, and an award for
feature writing. Bevo was returned safe to his pasture at the university, but soon retired from all official duties.

In November of 1954, Willie turned twenty. A month before, he
had written a column in anticipation of the milestone, in which he
prepared to "greet adulthood with varying degrees of disillusion,
cynicism, and apprehension." In his weekly "Round-Up" columns he
continued to write more thoughtfully and less lightheartedly about
campus life; his prose became leaner and the content more idealistic, with frequent references to Thomas Jefferson, Walt Whitman,
and William Faulkner. After the landmark Supreme Court decision *Brown v. Board of Education of Topeka, Kansas*, handed down in
May 1954, Willie took up the topic of school integration. Invoking

Celia Ann Buchan, 1956.

Hodding Carter Jr., Pulitzer Prize–winning editor of Greenville's *Delta Democrat-Times*, Willie made clear that he too was a proponent of integration, though he, like many southerners, believed "only a patient and comradely approach to the problem can be of permanent good." At the University of Texas, undergraduate classes (but not housing) would be integrated by the fall of 1956.

Then during the spring of Willie's junior year, he met Celia Ann Buchan. A year younger than he, Celia was a petite, sophisticated brunette with a heart-shaped face, from a well-to-do Houston family. At the university, she was enrolled in Plan II, the most prestigious course of study; beautiful as well as brainy, her sophomore year she had been elected Cowboy Sweetheart. She and Willie were introduced at a touch football game, and she was attracted by his "infectious gaiety. . . . He drew people to him whose spirits were heightened in his company, so our lives often felt more charged and delicious when he was around. . . . He was outrageous in an era when outrageousness was in short supply."

Also that spring, Willie put his name on the ballot for the editorship of the *Daily Texan*, the position he'd been eyeing ever since he'd arrived on campus. Although he had other sources of support, such as his friends in Brackenridge and his contacts in the journalism school, he turned to his fraternity to help get him elected. Dave Williams, president of Delta Tau Delta, became his campaign manager, and the nearly hundred members worked tirelessly, handing out brochures and hanging up posters around campus. With the Delts behind him, Willie won handily, in what the newspaper termed a "landslide." The election helped to cement his bond with his fraternity brothers, many of whom would remain lifelong friends.

"It was a viciously hot Texas afternoon in June when I moved my ten or fifteen favorite books, a toothbrush, an electric razor, an extra pair of shoes, and an emergency pint of Old Forester into the editor's office of *The Daily Texan*," Willie recalled in *North Toward Home*. Along with his other paraphernalia, he brought with him Joseph

Pulitzer's manifesto and tacked it on the wall: "That it will always fight for progress and reform, never tolerate injustice or corruption, always fight demagogues of all parties, never belong to any party, always oppose privileged classes and public plunderers, never lack sympathy for the poor, always remain devoted to the public welfare, never be satisfied with merely printing news, always be drastically independent, never be afraid to attack wrong, whether by predatory plutocracy or predatory poverty."

On June 7, 1955, the title *Texan* Editor appeared for the first time under Willie's byline. "A NEW YEAR begins today for the *Texan*," he wrote in his first editorial. "We've been ready." He was more than ready; he had polished his ideals and honed his writing skills. He assured his readers, "You will be jostled, cajoled, embarrassed. Yet, through our telescope of ideas, you will see your life here in much nobler focus." He disdained "the tragic shroud of indifference which cloaks our undergraduate" and "this student apathy." Vowing to report on state, national, even world news, he promised, "We will convince you to think. We will persuade you to know and to feel." And he forecasted: "When state demagogue or campus demagogue speaks slyly of press censorship, you will help us wage the fight." Finally, Willie could call the paper *his*.

Willie (left) and Ray Farabee, in April 1955, relaxing after Willie won the *Daily Texan* editorship and Farabee was elected student body president.

In the summer, the *Texan* came out only twice weekly. As incoming editor, Willie was in full charge, writing and editing stories—and proudly mailing the issues overseas to Celia, who was traveling in Europe, including to Oxford, England, a journey that, she later wrote, "would have lifelong repercussions." No doubt anticipating the long hours he would put into the newspaper during his senior year, Willie enrolled in three classes that summer—government, Spanish, and anthropology. During the academic year, he would take only three fall classes, economics, government, and the Poetry and Prose of Walt Whitman, and in the spring two literature classes, including Selected Plays of William Shakespeare. But that summer, there was still time to swim in nearby Barton Springs and to down a brew at Scholz Garten, the nineteenth-century beer garden located near campus.

Late that summer, Willie made the long trip to Yazoo City, this time driving his "ramshackle Plymouth," to visit family and friends. On reaching Mississippi, he "had the most overwhelming sense of coming *home*, to some place that belonged to me." He arrived during a historic moment, one that would prove to be a turning point for him as well. Shortly before the opening of that fall's school term, fifty-three black residents in Yazoo City, at the urging of the NAACP, had signed a petition to the local board of education requesting the immediate desegregation of the public schools. After the names of the petitioners had appeared in the newspaper, thirty-three of them had withdrawn their support, but still the controversy rattled the town.

On August 26, the Citizens' Council of Yazoo City sponsored a Friday-night meeting at the public grammar school on Grand Avenue. The local paper reported that the event was "highly successful" and that "men and women packed the auditorium." Willie was one of those present. That night the participants, his former neighbors and the parents of his friends, plotted retaliation against the petitioners, by evicting them from their homes and refusing to sell them groceries. About the experience, he would later write, "I knew in that instant, in the middle of a mob in our school auditorium, that a mere three years in Texas had taken me irrevocably, even without my recognizing it, from home." One week afterward, all but six of the petitioners had withdrawn their names. Nearly fifteen years would pass until the Yazoo City public schools integrated; when they did, Willie Morris would be there.

He soon returned to Austin to resume the editorship of the *Daily Texan*. It was a grueling schedule, with the paper due to the printer each night at 2 A.M. Willie's roommate at the Delta Tau Delta house recalls having to drag him out of bed to make his early classes. On September 18, Willie reprinted his goals for the newspaper, those he'd written the past June. But in early November, he wondered in print if he'd fulfilled his promises—that, perhaps, "the real things have gone unmentioned." Later that month, he celebrated his twenty-first birthday with Celia. He recalled, "We drank a quart of California wine, and for a birthday present she gave me a book of Victorian poetry, and with an unsteady hand and a big laugh she wrote on the flyleaf, 'Grow old along with me, the best is yet to be, the last of life, for which the first was made.'"

With the backing of several professors, that fall Willie applied for a Rhodes Scholarship to study at Oxford University. He did well in the regional exams and in early December left for the final interviews in New Orleans. On December 11, the *Daily Texan* announced that he'd won the coveted spot, one of just thirty-two in the country. He was the university's first Rhodes Scholar in a decade, and back home in Yazoo City the news made the front page of the paper. He commented: "Yet there were to be no congratulations, personal or formal, from the office of the President, or his army of administrative deans, and certainly none from the Board of Regents." The reason: at the *Daily Texan*, "unusual things had been happening."

Despite his misgivings that he might have "reneged" on important coverage, in Willie's editorials and columns he had written in favor of integration, extolling the Texans who'd taken a moderate stance; he'd come out against censorship of college newspapers and conformity in thinking; and he'd recounted the corruption in Governor Shivers's administration. As promised, he'd reported on state and national topics, in particular on a bill before Congress called Fulbright-Harris, which, if approved, would deregulate the natural gas industry. Proponents argued that the legislation would free producers to develop new sources of fuel, while opponents argued just as fiercely that higher prices for consumers would result. Willie editorialized against the bill, one of few Texas editors to do so.

The Board of Regents took exception to the *Texan's* editorial stances, especially when it came to Fulbright-Harris. One of the Regents, who himself held oil interests, was quoted in an Austin newspaper as saying, "We feel *The Daily Texan* is going out of bounds to discuss the Fulbright-Harris natural gas bill when 66 percent of Texas tax money comes from oil and gas." In the same article, he denied that the Regents were overreacting, saying, "We just want to hold [Willie] to a college yell." But the Board clamped down, ordering the newspaper not to discuss national and state issues and instituting earlier copy deadlines to give faculty sponsors more time to scrutinize editorials.

Willie and his staff immediately tested the new restrictions. On taking the editorial helm, he had reminded readers that their new editor was "a strong believer in a free, unhindered press," and that he hadn't forgotten that "the Yankees threw his great-grandfather's presses in the town well in 1863." Now he pushed back against university officials. He tried to publish a guest editorial from the *New York Times* against Fulbright-Harris, along with a column quoting Thomas Jefferson on freedom of the press, but both were censored. Willie appealed the decision to the student-dominated publications board, and the articles were later printed.

The dispute continued in the pages of the *Texan* during all of February and into March. As reason for the censorship, the Board of Regents cited a Texas law prohibiting state funds from being used to "influence the outcome of any election or the passage or defeat of any legislative measure." The Student Association's "attorney general," a law student appointed to consult with more than a dozen legal scholars, held that the law didn't apply to the *Texan.* Still, the dispute continued. When his commentaries were censored, Willie ran blank spaces with the headline "This Editorial Withheld" or wrote facetious essays entitled "Let's Water the Pansies" and "Don't Walk on Grass."

Through it all, Willie's newspaper received the support of the majority of the student body, many other college papers from around the country, and some local and national press. Ronnie Dugger, who'd started his own Austin-based paper, the *Texas Observer*, editorialized passionately in favor of the *Daily Texan.* J. Frank Dobie, folklorist, author, and a former professor at the university, also spoke

Willie with Celia at her sorority house, circa 1956.

out for the *Texan*, writing the Regents that they were "as much concerned with free intellectual enterprise as a razorback sow would be with Keats' 'Ode on a Grecian Urn.'" In March 1956, Willie published his first national article, in the magazine the *Nation*, outlining the position he'd taken on Fulbright-Harris and chronicling the censorship controversy. Ultimately, President Eisenhower vetoed the bill. But, Willie editorialized, "The issue is not how the *Texan* feels on the Fulbright-Harris bill. To believe so is to cloud reality. The issue is, should not a newspaper have the right to criticize the majority? Cannot a newspaper sometimes be the underdog?"

Finally, toward the end of March, the controversy abated. Willie's point of view had been buoyed by what the university had taught him about "the necessity of the free marketplace of ideas." The University of Texas would, he wrote, "teach those of us with good minds and small-town high school diplomas that we were intelligent human beings, with minds and hearts of our own that we might learn to call our own, that there were some things, many things—ideas, values, choices of action—worth committing one's self to and fighting for, that a man in some instances might become morally committed to honoring every manifestation of individual conscience and courage." Although Willie's tenure on the paper ended with an uneasy stalemate with the Regents, in April they put in place even more restrictive rules that would make it harder on subsequent *Texan* editors to exercise their right to a free press.

Meanwhile that spring, Celia Buchan was also making a mark on campus. The *Daily Texan*, under the alliterative banner headline "Charmin' Celia Cradles Campus Crown," reported in early April that she had been elected Sweetheart of the University of Texas. "Five thousand people sang 'The Eyes of Texas' to her in the gymnasium," Willie recalled in *North Toward Home*. The honor wasn't only an acknowledgment of Celia's "vivacious personality" and "impish smile and sparkling brown eyes," it was a recognition of her "knack for acquiring A's."

Back in Yazoo City, Rae and Marion Morris had worried about their son during that semester's drawn-out and highly public dispute over the editorial policies of the *Daily Texan*. But early that June Willie graduated from the University of Texas, taking his degree in English Literature with High Honors, and a Phi Beta Kappa key. He had become the campus leader he had hoped to be, and accolades had been heaped upon him. In the fall he would sail for England, and a much different student life at Oxford University.

FOUR

"Leaping and Lingering"

From Oxford to the *Observer*

───────────── ❖ ─────────────

It had been the freest time of my life, and I learned there something of
myself—my abilities, faults, convictions, prejudices.
—*Willie Morris*, My Two Oxfords

IN OCTOBER OF 1956, THE THIRTY-TWO RHODES SCHOLARS FOR
that year gathered in New York City to set sail on the sleek new ship
the *Flandre*, one of the largest vessels built in France since the end
of World War II. Even before the voyage got under way, Willie was
making new friends. The previous year, Edwin Yoder, editor of the
Daily Tar Heel, the student newspaper at the University of North
Carolina, had closely followed the censorship dispute at the *Texan*,
writing articles in support of Willie. After they were both selected
as Rhodes Scholars, Willie phoned him suggesting that they meet
in New York before the sailing date. In the historic Hotel Taft, north
of Times Square, Yoder spotted Willie for the first time, "a rather
bewildered-looking fellow in the lobby, staring up into vacancy." They
became friends immediately and would remain so for four decades.
"Brothers really," Yoder would write.

When the *Flandre* arrived at Plymouth, England, the scholars
were greeted by E. T. "Bill" Williams, who as Warden of Rhodes
House was director of the Rhodes Trust and scholarship program.
He put them aboard a train for the several-hour trip to Oxford.
Situated about sixty miles northwest of London, Oxford dates from
the tenth century. Two rivers wend their way through the venerable
city, the Thames (known locally as the Isis) along the west, and its

Willie (kneeling, front row, fourth from left) on the deck of the *Flandre* with
the other Rhodes Scholars for 1956.

narrower and calmer tributary the Cherwell on the east. In the early
1950s Oxford boasted a population of about a hundred thousand and
bustled with commerce—the sidewalks of its main street, the High,
were often jammed with shoppers and with students hurrying to
class in their black academic robes. On the roadway, Willie observed
"multifarious vehicles and grinding motors and the edgy berating of a
hundred horns, and wave upon wave of bicycles." He saw little shops
that seemed straight out of a Charles Dickens novel, "antiquarian
booksellers and numismatists and Indian art dealers and tiny tailor-
ing establishments."

Oxford University had its roots in the twelfth century. Its separate
colleges—when Willie studied there, they numbered nearly forty—
melded seamlessly into the lively cityscape, their gargoyled buildings fabricated from a local yellow limestone that lent them a warm,
honeyed glow. "Entering the gateways of the Oxford colleges," Willie
wrote, "one abruptly passes into another world. Six of the colleges
. . . abut on the High, and suddenly there they are, unhurried and
intimate and smug beside the noisome modern commerce . . . The
college gardens with their sweeping lawns and herbaceous borders
are magnificent in the waning afternoon."

Willie became a member of New College, which, he liked to remark, "had been new in 1379." He lived "in a little room there across from the old city wall, which was eleventh century, with the embattlements and the slots for arrows." He likened it to living in a museum, and an underheated museum at that. The dining hall of New College, he pointed out, was "older than the discovery of my own country." He breakfasted on oatmeal and kippers and dined on roast beef, Brussels sprouts, and potatoes, and felt far from home: "a long way, too long, from the Yazoo High cafeteria." He and fellow southerner Ed Yoder fantasized about heaps of turnip greens, fried chicken, and cornbread.

New College, Oxford University. Willie joked that it "had been new in 1379."

Willie felt the weighty heritage of the age-old university, where his august predecessors had ranged from the writers T. S. Eliot and Evelyn Waugh to the founders of Pennsylvania and of Methodism, William Penn and John Wesley, to Lawrence of Arabia and King Olav of Norway. He absorbed the dreariness of the English climate, which was overcast and chilly in the winter months. Later, he would write about his Oxford experience: "The sacrosanct privacy of the place, the perpetual fogs and rains, elicited a loneliness, an angst and melancholia such as I had never before known." But he approached even the weather with his characteristic humor, quipping one winter day: "Oh to be in April, now that England's here." To escape the gray chill, Willie would meet friends at the half-timbered Turf Tavern, an ancient alehouse set in a narrow, winding alleyway near the landmark Bridge of Sighs. They would socialize into the evenings, basking in the cheery fire and nursing the warm bitter beer for which English pubs are famous. The literary history of the Turf stoked Willie's imagination: Thomas Hardy supposedly used the pub as his model for the "obscure and low-ceiled tavern" in his novel *Jude the Obscure.*

Not long after his arrival in England, Willie received a transatlantic phone call, a rarity in those days. It was his father, calling to let him know that Skip had died. His parents had wrapped Skip in Willie's championship baseball jacket and buried him in their backyard, under a fragment of white marble on which they had carved *Skipper*. After the call, Willie wrote, "I wandered alone among the landmarks of the gray medieval town. A dozen chimes were ringing among the ancient spires and cupolas and quadrangles, all this so far in miles and in spirit from the small place he and I had once dwelled." Later, he sent a letter to his parents. "Why don't you all get another fox terrier? Call him Skipper II. I think it would be a very good idea."

Despite the scholars' difficulties in adjusting, "slowly, the spell of Oxford grew, until one was suffused with it, with its majesty and largesse," Willie wrote. "We became Oxford men." The usual Rhodes tenure was two years, but he became "so enamoured of that haunting, beautiful place that I wondered if I could ever muster the strength to leave." The university's signature teaching method, the tutorial, emphasized independent study and reading. Lectures were optional: "One of the English students explained to me that they had gone out of vogue with the invention of printing in the fifteenth century," Willie said. Oxonians read extensively in their chosen field, wrote one or two weekly essays, and met regularly with a tutor to discuss their work. Comprehensive examinations, both written and oral, were held at the end of the scholar's final year, lasting several hours a day for up to two weeks.

For his degree, Willie at first chose to read philosophy, politics, and economics, but soon he switched to history, which at Oxford meant mainly British history. In *North Toward Home*, he remembered the reception of his tutor, Herbert Nicholas, to his very first essay, on the electoral restructuring known as the Reform Act of 1832:

> I had stayed up straight through one fog-filled night applying the finishing touches. My next-to-last sentence said, "Just how close the people of England came to revolution in 1832 is a question that we shall leave with the historians." I read this to my tutor, and from his vantage point in an easy chair two feet north of the floor he interrupted: "But Morris, we *are* the historians."

By comparison to his hectic years at the University of Texas, Willie's time at Oxford was "quiet and detached." Yet while there he served as president of the American Association, contributed articles to the Oxford literary magazine, *Isis*, and played on the varsity basketball team, which won the national championship. He attended afternoon teas and sherries, champagne receptions, garden parties, and formal balls, but also get-togethers in his fellow students' rooms where they dined on pork pie and drank cheap red wine.

Willie with English friend and fellow Oxonian David Palmer.

Willie was appreciated by both American and British students for his gregariousness and wit. During the breaks between school terms, he and his friends traveled throughout the British Isles and the continent. Yoder recalled that Willie "carried his clothes and books in a worn old suitcase without a handle which he would hoist and carry on his shoulder." For one trip, they purchased an ancient Buick town car "almost as long as a hearse," for $150, for the drive to Paris and on to Rome. But the ramshackle car, christened "John Foster Dulles" after the much-traveled U.S. Secretary of State, couldn't get even as far as Dover and the English Channel ferry before blowing out two of its tires.

Back home, in the fall of 1957, Rae Morris began to feel unwell, and he consulted doctors in Jackson. In letters to his parents, Willie fretted about his father's health, pressing them for information. Later that fall, Rae was diagnosed with cancer, and Willie returned to the States to spend the Christmas holidays. He made the trip to Austin and visited Celia, who had graduated in the spring of 1957 and was working for a vice president of the university and teaching freshman English. By New Year's, she and Willie were engaged.

Willie went back to Oxford to finish his second year, but in the spring he received a transatlantic call from his mother, informing him that his father's health had worsened. Borrowing money from Bill Williams, the Warden of Rhodes House, he flew home. After visiting his parents, he spent most of that summer working for the *Texas*

Observer. Toward the end of August, he saw his father in the hospital in Yazoo City for what would be the last time. Willie badly wanted to tell Rae that if he ever had a son, he would name the boy after him, but he couldn't get the words out. Then late in the afternoon of August 30, at the Chapel of St. John the Divine Episcopal Church in Celia's hometown of Houston, Willie and Celia were married in a subdued ceremony. Mrs. Morris attended from Yazoo City along with Buba Barrier, who stood up as best man, while two friends from Texas, Ronnie Dugger and Bill Brammer, were ushers. Rae Morris passed away three days later, on September 2. His service was held at the First Methodist Church in Yazoo City, with the burial taking place in Glenwood Cemetery.

In October, the newlyweds sailed with the 1958 Rhodes class for Willie's third year at Oxford, which they would pay for themselves, because the Rhodes trustees didn't award stipends to married students. He found an apartment, with a pleasant view of the town, which would become a gathering place for their many friends. Celia had fallen in love with Oxford during her earlier visit, and she reveled in taking daily walks, sampling the local fare at the markets, and like Willie, frequenting the famous Blackwell's bookstore. She began taking tutorials in New College, in Greek tragedy. But the period following his father's death was difficult for Willie. Celia remembered that during the first year of their marriage, though he could still be outgoing with the other Rhodes Scholars, he had often lain in bed for hours, "his face to the wall." She felt grateful to him for bringing her back to Oxford, but she felt distant from him.

By the spring of 1959, Celia was pregnant and Willie had passed his arduous exams, earning a B.A. in history with second-class honors (the type of degree received by most Rhodes Scholars). By then, the trustees had relaxed the rules against Scholars marrying, so he was again eligible for a stipend. Deciding to stay in Oxford for a rare fourth year, he took tutorials in the history of the American South in the decade before the Civil War and in American-British diplomacy before World War II. That year, Willie and Celia lived "in a big dusty house on Norham Gardens," to the north of the University Parks and just west of the River Cherwell. It was "a top-floor flat with frayed Victorian rugs and a hole in the bathroom window" and with no telephone or refrigerator. On November 1, 1959, Celia gave birth

Willie with Celia, after he received his degree from Oxford University.

to their son, whom they named David Rae. Willie was present in the delivery room when the nurse pronounced the newborn "a big Texas man." Under the British health care system, Willie calculated, David Rae had cost them "82 cents"—and he wouldn't have been that expensive if Celia hadn't had a cold that required some medication. When Willie tried to telephone his mother about David's birth, "the English operator phoned back in half an hour and said, 'I'm sorry to tell you this place Yazoo City does not exist.'"

By May 1960, David Rae was crawling and it was becoming increasingly difficult to care for him in a third-floor apartment with few amenities. Willie, in addition to taking tutorials, was staying up nights writing a novel. He was, he later said, "waterlogged with the past." He corresponded with Hodding Carter Jr. about going to work for the *Delta Democrat-Times*, but there was no position available. When Ronnie Dugger wrote from Texas suggesting that he return to Austin to become editor of the *Observer*, Willie eagerly accepted.

And so the man that Ed Yoder has characterized as "easily the most celebrated and charismatic American Oxonian of his years" repatriated. After leaving the place that English poet Matthew Arnold termed the "city of dreaming spires," Willie would reflect: "It had been the freest time of my life, and I learned there something of myself—my abilities, faults, convictions, prejudices." He was ready, at last, to return to his native country, and to the fray of a job in journalism.

✦ ✦ ✦

On the way to Texas, Willie and his family stopped to sightsee at Hyde Park, Gettysburg, Harpers Ferry, and other historic places, arriving in Austin in early July. Celia found them a rental house on Bridle Path, in Tarrytown, a quiet neighborhood a few miles southwest of the capitol. With his name on the masthead as associate editor, Willie published his first article for the *Observer* on July 15, about the Democratic national convention in Los Angeles. He was returning to Texas at a stirring time, since presidential candidate John F. Kennedy had just picked Texas Senator Lyndon Johnson as his running mate.

Six years earlier, Ronnie Dugger had founded the *Texas Observer* as an "independent and liberal alternative" to the "hardcore right-wing newspapers" that predominated in the state. He had articulated the *Observer*'s manifesto this way: "We will serve no group or party but will hew hard to the truth as we find it and the right as we see

Ronnie Dugger in the offices of the *Texas Observer*.

it." Although the *Observer* had a circulation of only about six thousand, the weekly paper could be found on the desks of the governor and state legislators and in the Washington offices of the U.S. senators and congressmen from Texas, including Speaker of the House of Representatives Sam Rayburn. Lyndon Johnson, Willie learned, "underlined it with a ball-point pen."

Dugger had first noticed Willie when he was the "fighting liberal editor" of the *Daily Texan*. "That's what attracted me to Willie Morris," Dugger says. "He was what you'd call the inner-directed person; he was not submissive to authority because it was authority." For his part, Willie thought that Dugger was "not only one of the great reporters of our time in America; more than that, he had imbued an entire group of young and inexperienced colleagues with a feel for Texas, for 'commitment' in its most human sense, and for writing." He once remarked that Ronnie Dugger taught him how to be a reporter.

Willie began reporting on the presidential campaign. He attended a barbecue for Johnson in the little town of Blanco, where the candidate's mother had grown up. After the election, he covered Kennedy's visit to Johnson's ranch seventy miles west of Austin. Then in the December 16, 1960, issue of the *Observer*, Dugger wrote in a long article that "soon, Willie will become editor," while he himself would continue as contributing editor. Veteran journalist Robert Sherrill would become the paper's associate editor, the only other full-time writer.

Starting that January, the *Observer* shifted its focus to the fifty-seventh session of the state legislature. Willie chased lobbyists and lawmakers in the capitol, and after work retired a few blocks away to that other local institution, Scholz Garten, to build relationships over a beer with these same political players. In March, he assumed the title of editor, with Dugger passing him "absolute editorial control." Willie was responsible for writing thousands of words every week, as well as for supervising the paper's layout, creating the headlines, and proofreading the articles, in what he later said "was probably the toughest job I ever had."

Whenever the legislature wasn't sitting, the *Observer*'s small staff traveled throughout Texas, reporting on the political, literary, and social aspects of the Lone Star State. Willie put it this way: "Always there were the stories to cover, little unexpected events to describe, political clashes and small tragic happenings that no one would write about but us." He drove many miles, from the panhandle to the valley, from East Texas to West, pursuing the human interest story, his favorite kind of writing. He wrote about the poverty of the aged in Texas and the tradition of bullfighting over the border in Reynosa, Mexico. He profiled a county judge from Brownsville, Oscar Dancy, who worked tirelessly to improve local roads, though he himself didn't drive. Willie mulled where the South ended and the West began. Occasionally, he turned the spotlight on himself, such as when he reminisced about a trip to Paris during his Oxford days. Many of the articles and essays he wrote for the *Observer* would later serve as material for the Texas section of *North Toward Home*.

The two poles of Willie's Austin existence: the state capitol and Scholz Garten.

In liberal Austin, social life in the early 1960s was free-spirited. Reporters, writers, artists, politicians, and university professors would gather in one another's homes for drinks and barbecues, to discuss politics and literature. The *Observer's* shabby office in downtown Austin was a haunt of everybody from conservative Republicans to the visiting national press corps who came to cover Vice President Johnson's activities. Willie would often bring the reporters home; Celia now had a "new gang," she said, almost as interesting as the one they'd been part of in Oxford. But she felt the need for more purpose in her life, especially concerning her own career. She applied to graduate schools to study for a Ph.D. in English literature, and was accepted at both Columbia University in New York and Stanford

University in California; she was also awarded a Woodrow Wilson Fellowship. As for Willie, he had begun to feel that he had "run out of gas" putting out the all-consuming *Observer*. When Celia gave him the choice of where to relocate, Willie surprised her by choosing California.

Then one morning in early 1962, as he and Celia were having breakfast, a letter arrived from New York bearing the distinctive logo of *Harper's* magazine. Since Willie had recently completed an article for them, about the far right wing in Houston, this wasn't totally unexpected, but when he read the letter's contents he was surprised. John Fischer, *Harper's* editor-in-chief since 1953, was offering him a proposition: "Quite frankly I'm looking around for a successor. I don't know if you're the man, but I have a hunch that you are." Fischer didn't have a job opening, but said he would in three or four months. "You could try it up here for a while and see what you think," he suggested. "I'll do the same."

Fischer had been born in Texhoma, a city spanning the Texas-Oklahoma border. Like Willie, he was a Rhodes Scholar. He had followed Willie's path from the *Daily Texan* to Oxford University to the *Observer*, and he had read that newspaper closely, admiring Willie's work. Just as the *Daily Texan* had been a springboard to the *Texas Observer*, now the *Observer* was proving a springboard to *Harper's*. Willie, with his sense of history, was intrigued by Fischer's proposal: *Harper's*, debuting in 1850, was the oldest and one of the most prestigious magazines in the country, having published, among others, British writers Charles Dickens and Thomas Hardy and Americans Herman Melville, Henry James, Jack London, and Mark Twain. But, he explained to Fischer, they planned to move to California so Celia could study at Stanford. Fischer encouraged him to do that, and to "read, reflect."

Celia and David Rae left Austin before Willie, who stayed through November to cover the gubernatorial election. On November 9, his name appeared as *Observer* editor for the final time. By Christmas, he was in Palo Alto with his family. He briefly considered studying for a Ph.D. in history, but although he was accepted at Stanford he didn't receive financial backing, and so didn't have the resources to attend. Instead he audited some classes and did exactly as Fischer had suggested—he took time to read and reflect.

He also took some time to write, including some baseball reminiscences, which would appear in the *New Yorker* magazine in
November 1963 under the title "Memoirs of a Short-Wave Prophet."
He finished an essay comparing racism in Mississippi and Texas for
the leftist magazine *Dissent*, edited by Irving Howe, one of Celia's
professors at Stanford. When he wasn't writing, he spent time in the
public library poring over old issues of *Harper's*. He hung out with
a new friend, Bill Wyman, swapping sports anecdotes and attending
San Francisco Giants baseball games. Wyman was a former football
player (at West Point under assistant coach Vince Lombardi) who
was getting a Ph.D. in English Literature. "I would say Willie was
trying to find himself in California," Wyman says. "You remember
how they talk about 'leaping and lingering' in the ballad? I think here
Willie was lingering. He was gestating." "Leaping and lingering" is a
way of storytelling in which the ballad writer lingers over, or repeats,
part of the story, then abruptly leaps to the next part without a tran-
sition. During these disparate phases of Willie's life, he had experienced a period of great activity in Austin, sandwiched by relative
quiet in Oxford and California.

Willie once wrote, "All the important junctures in my life seem
to have involved buses." On a moonless spring night in 1963, Bill
Wyman carried his friend's suitcase and put him on a Greyhound in
San Francisco, this time bound for New York. Willie was on his way
to the most energetic and fabled chapter of his literary career. He was
twenty-eight years old.

FIVE

The Harper's Years

Reaching the "Organizational Summit"

There were eight million telephone numbers in the Manhattan directory, and every one of them would have returned my calls.
—*Willie Morris*, New York Days

WILLIE'S LONELY CROSS-COUNTRY JOURNEY TO NEW YORK TOOK him through Reno and Salt Lake City, Des Moines and Chicago. From the Windy City to New York City, the bus stayed on the turnpikes, stopping only at service plazas. Along the way, Willie observed his fellow passengers and stared out the window; he tried reading Bernard Malamud and Mark Twain, and when he lost concentration, he would "indulge in glamorous fantasies about the literary life of New York." After five grueling days, the Greyhound Scenicruiser pulled into Manhattan's chaotic Capitol Terminal on a "soft spring evening in 1963."

New York, New York. Even the name of the metropolis summons up its twin promises of glamour and possibility. For Willie, the city was a long way, in nearly every way, from home. He had come, like so many artists, musicians, and writers before him, to test his mettle. He had come like his hero Thomas Wolfe, whose protagonist in *You Can't Go Home Again* had moved to New York in search of fame as a writer. "We had always come, the most ambitious of us," Willie wrote in *North Toward Home*, "because we *had* to, because the ineluctable pull of the cultural capital when the wanderlust was high was too compelling to resist."

Willie with Celia on Park Avenue when he was working
for *Harper's*.

For many years Manhattan had been the center of the publishing industry, for the country and for the world, pouring forth books,
magazines and journals, and newspapers. An editor-in-chief of one
longstanding firm described the city as a "crossroads . . . a little like
living near an airport, noisy, frenetic, handy." Willie had an advantage
over many young aspirants: he was arriving in New York with the
job offer from *Harper's*. (He also interviewed at the book publisher
Random House, where he talked to a dismissive editor who made
him feel "the pluperfect hick," after which Willie vowed never to treat
anyone that way. In addition, the *New York Times* tried to recruit him
to run a new bureau in Dallas, but not wanting to return to Texas, he
turned it down.) Willie's annual salary at *Harper's* would be $6,500,
while the average family income in New York at the time was closer
to $8,000.

With Celia still in California, Willie began hunting for a place to
live. He'd had romantic notions of finding an apartment with a park

nearby for three-year-old David Rae, as well as a river view and a study, but he had to settle for a third-floor walk-up with two bedrooms, a master in the back and a smaller one for David Rae that looked out at the Empire State Building. The apartment was expensive, renting for a quarter of Willie's monthly salary, though it did have the advantage of being only a few blocks downtown from *Harper's*, whose offices were on East 33rd Street.

In July 1963, Willie Morris's name appeared for the first time in the magazine as associate editor. With real estate at a premium, his first office at *Harper's* was "approximately the dimensions of a good-sized dining room table," and he had to share the space with a secretary and a young manuscript reader. Willie's early responsibilities also entailed reading unsolicited manuscripts, known as "slush" in the publishing business. On occasion, John Fischer would send him out of the office to work with well-known public figures. Willie would attempt to pull articles from these potential contributors, such as former Central Intelligence Agency director Allen Dulles, who might be inexperienced writers despite their high accomplishments.

As soon as they could, Celia and David Rae joined Willie, and Celia resumed her graduate studies under Irving Howe, who had also transferred from Stanford to the City University of New York. But when their irascible landlord let garbage accumulate in the building's hallway and proved stingy with the heat, the family decided to move again. Celia found them another rental on 94th Street, on the Upper West Side, a neighborhood that at the time was "grungy and ravaged and down-at-the-heels." But the streets were less crowded than they were downtown, and life moved at a slower pace. Willie enjoyed upper Broadway's racial diversity, which reminded him of long-ago Saturday nights on Yazoo's Main Street. In this apartment, with his papers spread before him in a kitchen alcove, he took up writing what would become *North Toward Home*.

Willie said that, for him, the decade of the 1960s began in 1962, in the Palo Alto public library where he had gone to read back issues of *Harper's*. The decade had actually begun with a clear political break in the fall of 1960, when John F. Kennedy had defeated Richard M. Nixon for the U.S. presidency. At forty-three, Kennedy was the youngest man ever elected to that office, while his predecessor, Dwight D. Eisenhower, had been the oldest sitting chief executive in the nation's history. In his inaugural address, Kennedy had famously challenged Americans, "Ask not what your country can do for you, ask what you can do for your country." Within four months, the new president had founded the Peace Corps and had pledged to land a manned spacecraft on the moon. The ongoing financial recession improved under Kennedy, and the United States entered a period of growth that would last for most of the decade.

But as the sixties wore on, idealistic purpose was accompanied by social turmoil. In June 1963, civil rights activist Medgar Evers was murdered in the driveway of his home in Jackson, Mississippi; five months later, President Kennedy himself was assassinated in Dallas. In 1965, Black Muslim minister Malcolm X was gunned down in New York City. "The center was not holding," was how journalist and novelist Joan Didion characterized the chaos of the times. By 1968, there were half a million American troops in Vietnam, and at home the war was provoking violent protests and a generational chasm. Everywhere it seemed young people were in rebellion, and they showed it in their music, hairstyles, and clothing. That spring, Martin Luther King Jr. and Robert F. Kennedy were assassinated; in the fall, the conservative Richard Nixon was voted into office, promising to restore order and end the unpopular war, which nevertheless continued. Later, society would also be shaken by the movements for women's liberation and gay and lesbian rights, and the sexual revolution.

During these years, the cities seemed to be coming apart as well. Between 1964 and 1967, more than a hundred race riots erupted in cities ranging from New York to Birmingham and Los Angeles to Detroit. Each day on his way to work, Willie would see drug addicts and homeless people on the streets of Manhattan, trash piling up in the gutters, and graffiti covering the subway trains. He lived through the blackout of 1965, when more than 30 million people in the Northeast were without electricity, and through many strikes, which were becoming endemic to city life—transit strikes, newspaper strikes, garbage strikes, even a gravediggers' strike. Jarred by the city, at times Willie found New York claustrophobic and threatening. He took to calling it the Big Cave.

Soon after arriving, he was invited to his "first full-fledged literary cocktail party," which he primed himself for by rereading his Thomas

Wolfe, Sherwood Anderson, Sinclair Lewis, and William Faulkner, especially their highbrow adventures in New York. On a crisp fall night, in an imposing building on Riverside Drive, Willie recognized literary and art critics, book and magazine editors, playwrights and professors, and many writers, including the outspoken novelist and journalist Norman Mailer, who was occupying the center of attention. But Willie was disappointed when he, Celia, and a visiting friend from Texas were met by the literati with "frosty politeness."

Willie felt most comfortable in the company of other displaced southerners, both black and white, fellow "exiles" who were "alienated from home yet forever drawn back to it." He and Celia enjoyed socializing with the writers Ralph Ellison and Albert Murray, with whom they shared a love of history and family, a fondness for dogs and drink and the outdoors, a tendency to languid storytelling, their very "*Southernness.*" One New Year's Day, the three families got together for a traditional dinner of black-eyed peas and ham. Willie wrote: "Where else in the East but in Harlem could a Southern white boy greet the New Year with the good-luck food he had had as a child, and feel at home as he seldom had thought he could in the Cave?"

Willie had taken the job at *Harper's* with the expectation that he would become editor-in-chief when John Fischer retired. But the elder editor wasn't known for paying his writers well, and his magazine, Willie found, was at best "somewhat remote and docile and safe," at worst "grindingly arid." *Esquire* was more blunt about its competitor. In an article about New York publishing, its staff had labeled *Harper's* far from the "red hot center," stuck in "Squaresville." Nevertheless, Willie began training for his new duties. In New York publishing this was the era of the leisurely three-martini lunch, and so over drinks in little neighborhood restaurants or in the august Century Club, Fischer shared with Willie his knowledge of the business, both its financial and editorial aspects. To be a successful editor of a top publication meant making the rounds of business lunches and book launches, dinner and cocktail parties, and Willie gladly took on these responsibilities, becoming friendly with writers, some of whom he had been reading since his student days in Texas. At first he had found it hard to break into the New York literary world, which he described as "harsh" and "cliquish" and "mean as hell," but soon enough he worked his way into its red-hot center.

As early as 1965, Willie's editorial mark could be felt in the pages of *Harper's*. There were articles by Robert Sherrill, his colleague from the *Texas Observer*, about the Florida legislature, and by Ed Yoder, Willie's close friend from Oxford University, on W. J. Cash, author of *The Mind of the South*, a book Willie had read avidly while waiting for his Rhodes Scholarship interview in New Orleans. Pulitzer Prize–winning journalist David Halberstam reported on the war in Vietnam, and former congressional aide Larry L. King recalled his life as a "second banana" to Washington politicians. But during these early years at *Harper's*, Willie's greatest achievement was editing a special supplement called "The South Today . . . 100 Years After Appomattox."

One writer contributing to the supplement was novelist William Styron, another southern exile, whose work Willie had admired for many years. Styron had become famous in 1951 when, at the age of twenty-six, he had published his acclaimed first book, *Lie Down in Darkness*. He was a slow and painstaking writer who was then finishing his fourth novel, *The Confessions of Nat Turner*, about the slave who led a rebellion in Virginia in 1831. For *Harper's*, Styron wrote "This Quiet Dust," an essay explaining his long obsession with Turner, and Willie and Styron went on to become close friends. Other contributors included historian C. Vann Woodward, who wrote about the civil rights movement; novelist Walker Percy, writing about Mississippi; journalist Louis E. Lomax on returning to his Georgia hometown; and poet Langston Hughes. Willie supplied the foreword, in which he laid out his purpose, to "illuminate for non-Southerners the interaction of North and South." And so with this piece, Willie began his lifelong career of interpreting the South and southerners for his readers. Harper & Row would later publish the supplement in book form.

In April of the following year, 1966, Willie was promoted to *Harper's* executive editor. Although he still didn't have complete editorial or financial freedom, he published many nonfiction articles by major writers, including socialist Michael Harrington, economist Milton Friedman, anthropologist Oscar Lewis, and *Paris Review* cofounder George Plimpton. There was film commentary by Pauline Kael, biography by Nancy Mitford, an excerpt from *I Know Why the Caged Bird Sings* by Maya Angelou, as well as fiction by Philip Roth,

John Updike, and Isaac Bashevis Singer, and poetry by Robert Lowell and James Dickey.

But as Willie built his success at *Harper's*, there were strains on his marriage. His new job was all consuming, and although Celia was busy with her graduate studies, the daily responsibilities of their life fell on her. She accompanied David Rae to and from his school in Greenwich Village and made his play dates; she bought the family's groceries and took care of the laundry. "His life and mine were very different then," she explained later, in her autobiography. "And this was true for most men and women of our generation." At times, she wrote, she and Willie seemed like strangers to each other.

Willie and David Rae at N. D. Taylor School in Yazoo City. When Willie was invited home in April 1967 for National Library Week, he spoke at both the white and the black public schools.

Yet the marriage also had its happy times. Celia and Willie bought an old farmhouse seventy miles north of Manhattan, in the town of Patterson, New York. They loved the house, set on six acres among dogwood and crabapple trees, lilacs and peonies. During the summer, Willie commuted by train to his office, nearly five hours round trip. The family acquired a black Labrador puppy they named Ichabod H. Crane, after the character in Washington Irving's "The Legend of Sleepy Hollow." "Our new life seemed stable and full of promise," Celia wrote about that period, the mid-sixties.

In April 1967, Willie was invited to Yazoo City to speak during National Library Week. While there, he insisted on addressing not only the whites at Yazoo High but also the black students at N. D. Taylor School, a startling request for those segregated times and a provocation to some white townspeople, including his own mother. In his lengthy speech he talked about growing up in Yazoo City and about his new life in New York, but mainly about the common ground that existed between the races. "America is changing, and changing fast," he said. "You may not see it so much here in

Yazoo—indeed, I wish you could have been at the white high school yesterday when I spoke—but old patterns are crumbling. Perhaps someday, and it is my fervent hope, those of us of both races of the South will show America a way out of its impasse."

A month later, after four years at *Harper's*, Willie was finally named editor-in-chief, to be effective July 1. John Fischer announced his retirement and his protégé's promotion in the July issue, writing in his column, "The primary responsibility for editorial direction of the magazine passes into younger hands." They were much younger hands. Willie was only thirty-two, the youngest editor of the oldest magazine in America, and only the eighth editor in its history.

Two years before, *Harper's* had moved around the block into a stunning Art Deco building located at Two Park Avenue. Willie took possession of a corner office, once again hanging Joseph Pulitzer's manifesto on his wall. There was much work to do: he had been directed to revitalize the magazine by its new owners. In 1965, the book publisher Harper & Row had sold *Harper's* to a Minneapolis-based publishing conglomerate owned by the powerful and politically conservative Cowles family. John Cowles Jr., who'd been editor of the *Minneapolis Star* and the *Minneapolis Tribune*, had known and admired John Fischer for a long time; a decade before, Fischer had offered young Cowles a job as an editor at *Harper's*, but not wanting to relocate, he'd turned it down. Now the thirty-eight-year-old was president of the new corporation that owned *Harper's*.

Harper & Row had traditionally borne the magazine's annual six-figure deficit, but Cowles announced in an interview in the *New York Times* that he was "interested in making profits." He authorized Willie to increase the parsimonious fees *Harper's* had been paying to its writers—from a range of $300 to $600, to $2,000 to $3,000 per story. Higher fees would bring better writing, he and Willie believed, which would attract more readers and advertisers. But Willie knew that making *Harper's* financially viable wouldn't be easy, if it were possible at all. The yearly deficit when he took over was $150,000, and the circulation about 260,000. Postal rates and printing costs were rising, and subscriptions for serious general magazines were declining in favor of specialized publications focusing on single subjects such as sports or hobbies. Willie believed he was promised five years to turn the magazine around.

He immediately issued a public statement setting out the tone that his magazine would take. *Harper's* would be "lively and relevant if sometimes irreverent in attitude," and have "a stronger appeal for younger readers—young in age, young at heart." He began forming a vision of what this new *Harper's* could become—a "truly *national* magazine," he emphasized, with the best contemporary writing about the urgent social and political issues of that turbulent decade. Willie assembled a small staff of young writers that he called contributing editors: Larry L. King and David Halberstam, both of whom Willie had brought to the magazine when he had first gone there; *New York Times* journalist John Corry; and Marshall Frady, a southerner known for his biography of George Wallace. *Harper's* editor Robert Kotlowitz became managing editor and Midge Decter executive editor.

In addition to his contributing editors, Willie hired freelance writers, whom he "pursued relentlessly." One of his tactics for attracting the most talented freelancers was to contract with them between book projects and sometimes when their careers needed a boost. He proved to be an inspirational editor with a knack for matching writers with ideas. Larry L. King has written that Willie liked to get his contributors talking passionately about a topic and then say, "Write about that for me." John Corry explained Willie's gift as an editor this way. "Willie wanted you to write; he made you believe you could write. You wrote."

Besides working with authors, the editor-in-chief's job included overseeing the production schedule, page layout, and cover art; answering query letters from prospective writers; hobnobbing with other magazine editors and book publishers; and acting as the face of the magazine with the media. There were too many telephone calls to return and too many meetings and parties to attend. The pace was grinding, and as soon as one issue came out, it was time for the next to begin.

During its long history, *Harper's* had published poetry, book reviews, fiction, and nonfiction articles. In the sixties, nonfiction writing was evolving, and while still based on thorough reporting, articles were sometimes more personal; they also might use the techniques of fiction, such as description, dialogue, and first- or third-person narration. Willie gave his writers freedom to experiment, along with

Willie at his parents' house. This was an outtake from the author photo shoot for *North Toward Home*.

sufficient space to express themselves, and in his own writing, he himself was a practitioner of this New Journalism.

Shortly after Willie was promoted, he published *North Toward Home*. A two-part excerpt had appeared in the June and July issues of *Harper's* under the headline "A Provincial in New York: Living in the Big Cave." Despite the title, Willie no longer viewed the city as "the Big Cave," nor did he see himself as a provincial. "When the word got out in the New York rumorings that I was to be the editor-in-chief of *Harper's Magazine*, almost overnight, it seemed, I was one of them: 'they' became 'we.' And coy as this may seem, the difference was altogether remarkable: I began to feel that the city enveloped me, protected me, required more of me, almost in the way a small town does. I recognized now how much I had really come to love the city, and that I owed it something."

North Toward Home, which the publisher, Houghton Mifflin, labeled "an autobiography in mid-passage," won the distinguished Houghton Mifflin Literary Fellowship Award, given annually to promising but comparatively unknown authors. Economist John Kenneth Galbraith commented, "No one at age thirty-two should write his memoirs; Willie Morris is the only exception." The book was serialized in the *Saturday Evening Post*, illustrated with Hans Namuth's photographs of Yazoo City, and widely reviewed in national publications such as the *New Yorker*, *Time*, and *Newsweek*. Notices were mostly appreciative. Many critics, including the one for the *New York Times*, found the section on Mississippi to be the most successful, writing that "on the whole Morris gives us an appealing and affectionate portrait of a place able to engage the hearts of its people." The *Sunday Times* of London was more effusive, calling *North Toward Home* "the finest evocation of an American boyhood since Mark Twain." Willie received hundreds of fan letters from fellow southerners, telling him that he had given voice to their own feelings about their native region.

Down in Yazoo City, Willie would later write, the publication was "the biggest event to hit the town since the Civil War." While some Yazooans lauded the book, others were disturbed by his portrayal of them, including a classmate who wrote a front-page letter to the *Yazoo Herald* claiming that Willie had "through the medium of ridicule and exaggerations, deeply hurt my parents, and brought undue hurt and embarrassment to the school, church and friends." Willie replied to the *Herald* that he hoped in time the townspeople would "see my book for what it is: an evocation of a place and a period that I pray will endure in the hearts of others far removed from Yazoo, and hence an act of love." Meanwhile, New York toasted him with champagne parties and celebrated him in print and TV interviews.

"There were eight million telephone numbers in the Manhattan directory, and every one of them would have returned my calls," Willie wrote about his life as editor-in-chief. He was meeting not only prominent writers but also musicians, artists, Broadway actors, sports and film stars, including a few—Claudette Colbert, Alexis Smith—that he'd seen on the big screen in Yazoo's Dixie Theater back in the forties.

> I sat next to DiMaggio in the Garden ringside seats . . . I danced with Scarlett O'Hara's younger sister and Scott Fitzgerald's only daughter. I grew familiar with the palatial townhouses and high-rise

penthouses on the Upper East Side with marble staircases, wide and steep and long, and Steinway grands which Gershwin had played on right in these rooms, and Cole Porter of Peru, Indiana, and Johnny Mercer of Savannah, Georgia, and I talked with the people who had known them all.

Willie and his stable of writers met regularly for "after-work gossip and plotting" at the unprepossessing Empire Chinese Restaurant, near the *Harper's* offices, and later on at the tonier Elaine's bar and restaurant on the Upper East Side. They socialized over "interminable cocktails in the dying late afternoons," but informal publishing deals also were struck. Of this period, Willie said, "I drank too much, ate too much, talked too much."

Only two months after taking over at *Harper's*, in the September 1967 issue, Willie brought out an excerpt from William Styron's long-awaited *Confessions of Nat Turner*. Just to publish the celebrated Styron was a coup, but the piece ran to forty-five thousand words, the length of some books. The price Willie paid was also notable. He had intended to offer Styron $7,500, but at the insistence of John Cowles, he increased the amount to $10,000, as part of their plan to acquire the best contemporary writing.

Willie managed another publishing coup with Norman Mailer's "Steps of the Pentagon," described on the magazine's cover as "a documentary report about the famous Washington weekend during which thousands of Americans marched across the Potomac in the name of peace, and some—the author among them—ended in jail." Willie thought Mailer "a literary genius," and as an apprentice editor he had tried to publish him in *Harper's*, but John Fischer had rejected the submission. After the Pentagon march, which had taken place in October 1967, rumors had circulated that Mailer planned to write about his participation. Cowles agreed that Willie would offer $10,000 for a ten-thousand-word article. When Mailer's account grew to ninety thousand words, Willie made the unprecedented decision to publish it not in installments, but as nearly a hundred pages in the March 1968 issue.

"The Steps of the Pentagon" was at the time the longest article ever published in any magazine, and drew more letters than any other in *Harper's* history. Written in the New Journalism style, with

Willie signing a copy of *North Toward Home* soon after publication.

Mailer referring to himself in the third person, it pushed language to its limits, including the use of four-letter words. "'The Steps of the Pentagon' was in every aspect an affirmation of my dream for *Harper's*," Willie wrote, "bringing together as it did the artistic sensibility with the trustworthy eye for detail and event in a palpable moment passionate and important for the civilization." Later published as *The Armies of the Night*, it won both the Pulitzer Prize and the National Book Award.

Eight months later, Mailer wrote about the 1968 presidential conventions, in another controversial, award-winning, and lengthy article, which became the book *Miami and the Siege of Chicago*. Along with Styron, Mailer was instrumental in moving *Harper's* away from the "arid" magazine it had been, to one that took up important social and political issues and was decidedly in vogue. According to executive editor Midge Decter, "Under the editorship of Willie Morris, a Mississippi boy bred on the love of serious literature, *Harper's* had virtually overnight been turned into a writers' magazine and was in the process of becoming what is called in the trade a 'hot book.'"

For the next three years, *Harper's* would consistently publish articles that, in Willie's words, "aroused, interested, and engaged" its readers. One was Gay Talese's profile of the *New York Times*, issued in two parts in 1969, which became the bestseller *The Kingdom and the Power*. Another was Bill Moyers's "Listening to America," chronicling his journey across the country, which Willie and David Halberstam had suggested he make; the story was also the basis for a best-selling book and a Public Television series. Willie himself wrote a long, well-received article for the magazine, titled "Yazoo . . . Notes on Survival," about the integration of the Yazoo City public schools. In the piece, which became the cover for June 1970, he blended personal information and in-depth reporting in a style that would become his signature.

From time to time, the magazine would publish an article that profoundly changed the way the nation thought about an important issue. This was the case with Seymour M. Hersh's May 1970 article "My Lai 4: A Report on the Massacre and Its Aftermath." Nearly two years before, American soldiers had killed hundreds of unarmed civilians in the Vietnamese village of My Lai. Hersh interviewed more than fifty of the soldiers in order to tell the full story for the first time, winning the 1970 Pulitzer Prize for his reporting. Years later, Willie would comment that Hersh's article was one that he felt most proud of publishing. Veteran journalist Ronnie Dugger believes that, considering *Harper's* extensive coverage of Vietnam, "More than any other journalist, with the exception of Walter Cronkite, Willie Morris helped change public opinion about the war."

In 1971, *Harper's* devoted most of its March issue to Norman Mailer's "The Prisoner of Sex," his combative analysis of the women's movement. The controversial article would go on to sell more copies on newsstands than any other in the magazine's history. But shortly after its appearance, in late February, Willie was summoned to Minneapolis to meet with *Harper's* owner John Cowles Jr. Also present at the meeting were other executives, including William Blair, who had joined *Harper's* as president and publisher about a year after Willie had been named editor-in-chief. Against Willie's better judgment, Blair had been conducting readership polls to help determine the magazine's content.

For more than a month, Willie and Blair had been exchanging confidential memoranda about the magazine's persistent deficit. On February 17, Willie had sent Blair a mostly temperate six-page memo addressing Blair's suggestions for proposed cutbacks. "We are anxious to do all within our power to reduce expenditures in a sensible and realistic manner that will not do damage to the reputation and quality of *Harper's*," he assured the publisher. The staff, he went on, would "make every continuing effort to reduce our costs to the bone."

Specifically, Willie agreed to eliminate one position and to economize on secretarial staff; to cut editorial pages by 10 percent; and to shrink office space by half. To Blair's suggestion that they fire either the managing or executive editor, Willie proposed instead that he and Blair each slash their salaries by one-third. (Blair did not agree.) He wouldn't dismiss the contributing editors, which he believed would be a "very false and misleading economy. The contributing editors," he continued, "have been in many ways our editorial core and have consistently given *Harper's* the flavor and the color which it now has . . . and I do not think they have been overpaid." He also refused to consider transforming *Harper's* into a specialty magazine, since he believed that the "four alternatives offered as blueprints for *Harper's* future mean either another magazine entirely or none at all." He made clear that "I will never, under any circumstances, acquiesce in its death, whether it is a slow death or a sudden one. . . . [I]f I do not defend the survival of a *Harper's* that remains essentially the magazine that it is now, I will be grossly negligent to my duty and to the tradition I inherited." In concluding, he sounded a more conciliatory note:

> I will do everything I can to help save us money, to reduce John's deficit, and to make *Harper's* last. If we fight for our magazine's survival, as a *national* magazine, and a good one it now is, we will have upheld our responsibility to John to make and hold for him a viable entity that he can, if he chooses, at some later time merge or sell as he wishes. This is something we owe him deeply. I hope our future sessions will lead us to a way of satisfying this responsibility. This is our real obligation to our writers, our public, and our owner.

Now in Minneapolis, over the course of three and a half hours, Cowles and Blair and the other executives read Willie a

Willie in his office at *Harper's* a few months before his
resignation. (Photo courtesy of the Associated Press.)

twenty-one-page memo reiterating their point of view. The "magazine had caught on only with 'Eastern communicators,'" Blair told
him. Another businessmen commented, "No wonder it's such a failure. Who are you editing this magazine for? A bunch of hippies?"
Willie hadn't been asked to resign, but on March 1 he wrote a letter
of resignation to Cowles, effective March 15.

In the passionate, two-page letter, he said, "This has been an agonizing decision, but under the circumstances I feel I have no other
choice. I have been working for *Harper's* for eight years. I have taken
the responsibility of editing the magazine seriously and faithfully,
and . . . I believe quite firmly that we have published a magazine true
to its own finest traditions, and one that we can rightly be proud of."
He went on to complain bitterly about Blair, whom he characterized
as "a cloud of doom and defeatism." And he concluded: "We could

live with reduced budgets and lower expenditures across the board, as I mentioned in my memorandum of February 17, and indeed our editorial expenditures relative to the business side of our operation gives me no cause for guilt, but I cannot continue to devote myself to a magazine already defeated and dead, with only the date of the funeral unresolved." In a later statement to the press, Willie was more succinct. "It all boiled down to the money men and the literary men. And, as always, the money men won."

After Cowles accepted Willie's resignation, most of the *Harper's* staff resigned in protest. Other writers also rallied around Willie. Three Pulitzer Prize winners, the novelist William Styron, playwright Arthur Miller, and historian Arthur M. Schlesinger Jr., sent a telegram to Cowles asking that Willie be reinstated. Many others joined in praising Willie's contribution to the magazine, including James Jones, Gay Talese, Tom Wicker, and John Kenneth Galbraith. In protest, many of these writers and others pledged not to publish in the magazine again.

The *New York Times*, reporting on the dispute, called it "acrimonious and complex." It was a fair appraisal, and many years later Willie, his staff, and others were still trying to make sense of what had happened. In her memoir, *Harper's* executive editor Midge Decter suggested that Willie "had not properly taken the measure of the owner, who was in many ways a foolish man, and in no way more foolish than his totally impossible ambition for the magazine to be profitable."

In all, it had been a difficult few years. Even before the trouble at *Harper's*, Willie's marriage to Celia had unraveled, and in 1969 their divorce had become final. "We should never have gotten married," Celia believes. "We were just ideas to each other. Whatever went wrong with our marriage, it was just as much my fault as it was his." David Rae had continued living with his mother, and Willie had rented an apartment across the street from his office. "Nothing lasted," he wrote. "It all seemed in character with the American Sixties."

Willie would leave the city as he had come to it, without much money, and with a feeling that he didn't belong there. "Almost overnight years before I had suddenly felt myself a 'New Yorker,' and now, just as swiftly, the city became large and hostile again." The decade of the sixties, for Willie Morris, was finally over.

SIX

Self-Exile on Long Island

"Molding from This Another Life"

———— ⬥ ————

You are the best editor that *Harper's Magazine* has ever had in all its long
and venerable history. But these things we put behind us. You are also a
wonderful writer, which everyone knows, particularly me.
—*Letter to Willie Morris from James Dickey,
United States Poet Laureate, 1966–68*

SPRING COMES LATE TO THE HAMPTONS, ON THE SOUTH FORK
of Long Island, about a hundred miles east of New York City. In
March, the month that Willie arrived, temperatures linger in the forties during the day, and snowfalls are still common. He had first seen
the Hamptons from the window of a bus while on his way to the
easternmost Long Island town of Montauk to attend a meeting for
Harper's. On that visit, as he took in the historic villages and especially the flat land with its long rows of scrubby potato plants, he was
struck by the similarity to the Mississippi Delta, and he thought that
one day he might return there to live.

After resigning from *Harper's*, Willie moved out of his Midtown
bachelor's apartment. In Elaine's restaurant in Manhattan, he had
met Muriel Oxenberg Murphy, a wealthy, pretty socialite who'd been
a founder of the Department of American Paintings and Sculpture at
the Metropolitan Museum of Art. In 1969 they had begun a romantic
relationship, and Willie had often spent weekends at Muriel's home
overlooking Georgica Pond in the Hamptons town of Wainscott.
Now he settled in a wing of the large house, where in the evenings, at
the beginning of his "headstrong, self-inflicted exile," he would play

the gospel music of New Orleans–born singer Mahalia Jackson on the stereo, alternating with a reading of General Robert E. Lee's farewell address to the Confederate troops. Willie described his mood this way:

> In the snowy solitude I surveyed the frail wreck of ambition. The telephone never rang. I missed the perquisites and attentions of high station. It was strange to wake up in the morning and have no place, no office, to go to, no salary to pay the bills. I had come to New York with a heart full of stars and hopes, and to have gone so high so fast, then down in a moment, was more than I had ever bargained for, as if I had somehow lost my reason for existing. I gazed interminably out the window upon the hushed landscapes, the frozen inlet, the Canada geese in V formation, trying to put things into some larger piece. To try to figure out anew who I really was, and to begin molding from this another life, was baffling and mysterious.

Willie may not have recollected his telephone ringing, but to Ed Yoder, who spent a week in Wainscott with his old friend later that spring, it seemed to ring all the time. "People were calling every 10 minutes," he remembered, "to offer contracts and deals." Job offers also came by mail and occasionally by telegram. Colorado College, Southern Methodist University, and Duke University proposed visiting faculty positions. Robert Sargent Shriver Jr., John Kennedy's brother-in-law, invited Willie to dinner to talk about becoming head speechwriter for Maine senator and soon-to-declare Democratic presidential candidate Edmund Muskie. There were scores of other offers—to write for newspapers and magazines, attend symposia, serve on advisory panels, speak at workshops and commencements. The media petitioned him for interviews, and shaken *Harper's* subscribers sent him fan letters. Much of this correspondence remained unanswered as Willie, dejected and second-guessing what had happened at the magazine, pondered what to do next.

In Yazoo City, his mother worried about him. Toward the end of March she pleaded in a letter, "Please, Willie, tell me something of your plans. Don't shut me out." In early April she asked, "Have you gone into seclusion somewhere?" Willie left some of her letters unopened. But Bill Moyers, a friend and former *Harper's* contributor, told him something that resonated. When Moyers had left his job as publisher of *Newsday* in 1970, Willie had suggested he make his cross-country journey and write "Listening to America." Now Moyers returned the advice, reminding Willie that he was still young, and that he "still owned a typewriter." Willie decided to turn down all the job offers. "I thought about newspaper work again and other magazines," he wrote, "but I had had my organizational summit. I had given all of myself to my magazine, and I felt there was nothing else comparable for me in an institutional way."

What would he do? Ever since coming to New York he had juggled two careers, those of editor and writer. Now he decided that he would simply write: "I said to myself, 'Just try to go on with your own work and dedicate yourself to that and see what happens.'" Perhaps he had known all along that he was meant to be a writer, at least ever since he'd declared his intention to the young couple at the University of Texas whose book-lined home he'd visited one long-ago evening.

In spring 1971, the lengthy article that Willie had written about the integration of Yazoo City's public schools was published by Harper's Magazine Press as *Yazoo: Integration in a Deep-Southern Town*. The book, an updated and expanded version of the article, was well received by critics, with Dan Wakefield writing in the *New York Times*: "It succeeds, I think, because it is not only the story of Yazoo and Mississippi and the black-white battle in this society, but also because it is the story of Willie Morris, and the hopes and anguish of his personal history, which are intertwined with those of the place from which he came, and the place where he arrived." Psychiatrist and Harvard professor Robert Coles captured Willie's gift for this New Journalism technique when he wrote him, "You somehow bring contemporary social and cultural and political issues to life through a marvelous autobiographical way of letting things sift through yourself, and come out fresh and clear." Willie traveled to promote the book, especially throughout his native state. *Yazoo* soon sold out its first printing and went back to press.

In the fall of that year, Willie published his third book, *Good Old Boy: A Delta Boyhood*. Back in 1967, a few months after the publication of *North Toward Home*, he had gotten a letter from the renowned children's book publisher at Harper & Row, Ursula Nordstrom, who had edited such classics as E. B. White's *Stuart Little* and Maurice

Sendak's *Where the Wild Things Are*. She congratulated Willie on his memoir and reminded him of an earlier correspondence. "I hope you will remember that long before you wrote it and became rich and famous I asked you to write a book for this department. You said you might, and mentioned stories you might like to write about your dog. One of the things I especially loved personally was the fact that you had smooth fox terriers. I had a great one in my youth and there has never been anything like her since. Or if not about your dog, a book about a good old boy growing up—from ten or eleven to fourteen or so . . . in Mississippi. . . . *Good Old Boy* would be a good title." Willie had always held a special fondness for young people, and writing a book for adolescents appealed to him. He would return to his childhood in Yazoo City, but cast it as fiction, with the town's legends inspiring the fantastical plot and his friends the characters.

Willie had begun work on the manuscript while still at *Harper's*, and by October 1970, Nordstrom had reviewed a first draft, with the working title *Good Old Yazoo Boy*. She commented in a letter to Willie's literary agent, Joan Daves: "It has marvelous things in it. . . . I think that with a very little more effort on his part it can become a book that will live for a very long time." Among her suggestions, and those of his agent (who counted six Nobel laureates among her clients), were to include "SOME thoughts about the race situation during his boyhood," to clarify the time sequence and the children's ages, and to give the book more structure, with a "beginning, a real middle or turning point, and a real end." During the spring and summer of 1971, on Long Island, Willie made changes to the manuscript and the typeset galleys to carry out these recommendations. The book was dedicated to Muriel Oxenberg Murphy and her young daughter, Julia. In the foreword, he addressed David Rae, who had asked his father what life had been like in the South when he was growing up.

Good Old Boy was published to favorable notices, including from *Time*, the *Christian Science Monitor*, and the *Saturday Review*. *Time* described a tall tale "drenched in crawdads, squirrel dumplings, Delta woodlands, and Peck's-bad-boy jokes. But," the reviewer continued, "Morris eases out of realism into fantasy and back with no strain, and it's nice to think that somebody more contemporary than Huck Finn could remember it all that way." Willie's mother was pleased with the book, writing him, "I cried when I read many parts of it because it

The house on Church Lane in Bridgehampton, where Willie lived for seven years.

brought back memories of happier days." *Good Old Boy* won the Steck-Vaughn Award from the Texas Institute of Letters for best children's book and would become one of Willie's most-loved stories. For years he would receive packets of letters from schoolchildren about the escapades of his characters— spunky Rivers Applewhite, rebellious Spit McGee, a tribe of giant warriors, and the witch of Yazoo, whose local legend he embroidered. In 1988, *Good Old Boy* would be made into a TV movie by the Walt Disney Company and PBS, though the title was changed to *The River Pirates*. "Watching the filming of the L.A. boy playing me, and the others acting my boyhood chums such as Henjie Henick . . . was *déjà vu* of the most impressive kind, and exceedingly strange," Willie would write about visiting the set in Natchez. "They were ghosts for me in sunlight."

Willie lived in several places on Long Island's South Fork before settling in Bridgehampton. Founded in 1656, the town was home to about a thousand year-round residents, including a sizable black population, whose presence (in addition to the flat cultivated fields) reminded Willie of the Mississippi Delta. He liked the unpretentiousness, the white-painted churches and old graveyard. For seven years, he would rent a house on tree-lined Church Lane. Set back from the road, next to a potato field, the house was charming, with a wrap-around porch, a grape arbor, and an ample backyard.

He started his habit of sleeping late and writing during the afternoons. After finishing work for the day, he would often drop by Bobby Van's bar and restaurant. Bobby, who had studied music at the Julliard School, presided over the establishment from his baby grand, playing the standards of Irving Berlin and Cole Porter. With dark-paneled walls, Tiffany-style lamps, and red tablecloths, Bobby Van's became, according to a book about the area, "the watering hole that served as a kind of club for the country's best-known writers." Willie would frequently be joined by John Knowles and Truman

Willie in his study on Church Lane.

Capote, Peter Matthiessen and Joseph Heller, Kurt Vonnegut and Irwin Shaw, Betty Friedan and Jean Stafford, among other writers. Later on, James Jones would also be among them.

Still, Willie spurned the notion that Bridgehampton was a "writer's community," describing it instead as a convivial scene where friends who happened to write often got together, though they didn't "talk about writing all that much." Besides writers and artists, he liked hanging out with truck drivers and potato farmers, firemen and carpenters. David Rae, soon to be a teenager, visited from Manhattan during school vacations, and Willie enjoyed the company of his son and his young friends, taking them to ball games, performing card tricks, and entertaining them with stories about Yazoo City. He read them his manuscript for *Good Old Boy*, and delighted in working in some of their suggestions.

During this period, Willie was generally animated and social, but he could also be withdrawn. In October 1971, his mother complained in a letter, "You never answer your telephone anymore." In fact, he had started keeping his phone in the refrigerator, or worse for the

Willie with Marina and Bobby Van at their wedding in April 1975.

instrument if he happened to forget, in the oven. Another person trying unsuccessfully to contact him was his ex-wife, Celia, who wrote protesting that he was late paying alimony and child support. Willie could also be distant from old colleagues. David Halberstam wrote him, worried "that you had, in a time which was bad for you, closed yourself off from your friends. You simply are not allowed to do this; friends come for the bad times as well as the good."

In the winter of 1971–72, Willie was about to embark on a new book, a novel for adults. In 1969, he had signed a contract to write the novel for the distinguished publishing firm Alfred A. Knopf and the legendary Robert Gottlieb, who had edited Joseph Heller's *Catch-22*, among many other celebrated works of fiction and nonfiction. The manuscript was due to be completed by July 1972, and so during the "drab and snowy wintertime" Willie began writing about the up-and-down Washington career of the beautiful University of Mississippi graduate Carol Hollywell.

By January he was deep into her story, and Gottlieb wrote him, "The book sounds terrific, because it sounds as if it's coming out of you and yet controlled by you." In a letter to Bill Styron, Willie declared, "I've promised myself I'm going to master this form [fiction] if it kills me, and if this one doesn't hit the mark I'll keep on plugging away until they put me in the black earth of ol' Miss'ippi.

I'm learning just what an agony the act of the imagination can bring down upon you."

In April, Gottlieb reviewed the draft and delivered difficult news. "I know how painful it's been—but I also know how serious you are, which is why I fought with my impulse to go easy on you." He praised Willie for "not reacting defensively or offensively but only seriously. Which only reinforces my certainty that you will be a first-rate novelist." He urged Willie to round out his heroine's character, to "*fill* [the novel] with reality—episodes, actions, the way things are. Carol is a large enough conception to hold it all." A month later, Willie wrote to a Yazoo acquaintance that the novel "drags along and drags me with it." That fall he finally finished the revisions and wrote a shared dedication to his mother and Ed Yoder, who called the tribute "about the greatest honor ever to come my way" and "the highest expression of a great friendship."

Shortly after arriving in the Hamptons, Willie had begun seeing Barbara Howar, a talk show host and Washington insider who was writing her own book, a memoir. When both books were published in the spring of 1973, some reviewers noted that Howar's life story resembled that of Willie's heroine. Her *Laughing All the Way* made the bestseller list, but Willie's *The Last of the Southern Girls* disappointed critics, with the exception of Jonathan Yardley in the *New Republic*, who called the novel "great fun." The *New York Times* allowed that "Morris writes fine dialogue" but found the book only "serviceably written with a kind of tepid elegance." Two decades later, in 1994, Willie would admit in the Author's Note to the paperback edition that while writing the novel he had been "severely discombobulated." In addition to everything else he had gone through—divorce, leaving a job he'd loved, moving, separation from his son, and two turbulent romances—David Rae's black Labrador, Ichabod H. Crane, whom Willie had "kidnapped" from Celia and David, had been run over on Long Island.

Willie toured to promote *The Last of the Southern Girls*, which attracted widespread media coverage. Despite the novel's negative reviews, it achieved some financial success, chosen as a selection of the Book-of-the-Month Club, serialized in *Ladies' Home Journal*, licensed to a British publisher, and optioned for the movies (though never produced). Willie's publisher at Harper & Row, Ursula

Nordstrom, had been speaking facetiously when she had said that his writing had made him rich, but *The Last of the Southern Girls* did help Willie get "through alimony, child support, and the school bursar."

In Mississippi, Willie's grandmother Mamie had been in declining health for several years, and on February 15, 1974, she died in a nursing home in Yazoo City. Marion Harper Weaks was buried in Raymond, Mississippi, next to her husband, Percy, who had died twenty years before. Willie and David Rae attended her funeral. "She was 97, the repository of vanished times for me," Willie wrote. "Although she would not have understood had I told her, she helped me to have feeling for the few things that matter. I was nourished in the echoes of her laughter."

But after *The Last of the Southern Girls*, Willie didn't give up on writing fiction. In August 1973 his new literary agent, Sterling Lord, who was well known in publishing circles for representing the Beats writers Ken Kesey and Jack Kerouac, sold to Knopf a second novel of Willie's, to be called *The Chimes at Midnight*. Ever since his days at Oxford University, Willie had been haunted by the novel's premise, inspired by the misfortune of an English friend who had fallen and permanently injured himself one night while climbing over the old city wall.

The manuscript had been due to Knopf in September 1974, but in December Willie laid the project aside. Bob Gottlieb wrote him that he was "grateful that you're doing what I'm sure is the right thing . . . and scared, because it *is* scary to advise someone like you to take such a step. Particularly when the advice is taken." In the spring of 1975, Willie turned his attention to another novel, *Taps*, which had also been in his mind for a long time. Recalling his own adolescence, the story would be about a sixteen-year-old southern boy who plays "Taps" at the funerals of returning Korean War veterans.

During these years, Willie wrote occasional magazine and newspaper articles to help support himself. Among them were "The Lending Library of Love" (about relationships between men and women) for *Newsweek* and "Bridgehampton: The Sounds and the Silences" for the *New York Times*. He also contributed a lengthy introduction to a picture book called *A Southern Album*, which was published by Oxmoor House in 1975. Editor-in-chief John Logue was thrilled with what Willie turned in, describing it as "a lightning bolt" that "will surely break every other heart in the South." *Publishers Weekly* and *Library Journal* praised the book, as did the *Christian Science Monitor*, which found the introduction "perceptive and stirring." But the prestigious *New York Times Book Review* savaged the project and labeled Willie's contribution "derivative drivel" and "foggy Faulkner."

Willie had a policy of not reading reviews, good or bad, but he reluctantly bought a copy of the newspaper and read this one. The raw criticism and personal tone disturbed him, so much so that three years later he addressed it in his next book. "The piece attacked me for greed, self-importance, and a lack of character, and said my well had run dry. It added that I did not understand the South. Not understand the South, indeed!" But when he read the review to his good friend James Jones, who had himself been on the receiving end of spiteful criticism, Jones only giggled. Willie concluded, "A serious writer must grow, mature, live, and survive with his work—some good, some bad, some great—the old rhythms." Jones advised Willie to put the review behind him and get on with his writing.

Willie had met Jim Jones in New York City during the 1960s. In 1951, Jones had published his first novel, *From Here to Eternity*, which had won the National Book Award. He had lived for a long time in Paris and then briefly in Florida, before Willie persuaded him to move to Long Island. In the summer of 1975, Jones and his family bought an old farmhouse in Sagaponack, which Willie nicknamed "Chateau Spud" because it sat next to a potato field. Despite their age difference of nearly fifteen years, the two men became like brothers. Willie liked the older man's straightforward approach to life, appreciated his talent, and plain enjoyed his company. The way he spoke even reminded Willie a little of his own father. As for Jones, "My father just adored [Willie]," his daughter, Kaylie, remembers. During the next two years Jones, who suffered from a heart condition, would strive to finish *Whistle*, the final novel in his World War II trilogy. Willie, meanwhile, was still trying to find his novelist's voice, working intermittently on *Taps* and *The Chimes at Midnight*. He recalled: "Often at night around the long table in the kitchen we would read to Gloria and to each other—'just trying things out a little,' as he would say."

Willie in the kitchen at Chateau Spud, in front of a painting of James and Gloria Jones.

Over time, Willie grew close to the entire Jones family—Jim's wife, Gloria, and their children, Jamie and Kaylie. They celebrated holidays together, cooked hamburgers on the beach, and played Monopoly and other games. "At Chateau Spud there would be spaghetti or Chinese or *choucroute* dinners with Italian wine, hunkering down for hurricanes, poker games every Tuesday night, and TV-watching around the kitchen table," Willie wrote. He also delighted in staging pranks on the unsuspecting Joneses, similar to the ones he'd pulled on his neighbors in Yazoo City. On the telephone he once fooled Gloria into believing that he was a highway commissioner and that a crew would be arriving the next day to construct a road through their backyard. One winter night when she was a teenager, Kaylie playfully asked Willie if he would be her godfather, and she, Willie, and Jim drew up a paper for all three to sign. But as her father's health worsened, Kaylie says, Willie took his role more seriously, even escorting her to visit colleges during her senior year of high school.

Willie and the Joneses also shared a love of softball. An annual fundraising game had long been held in Bridgehampton among artists, and in the sixties and seventies, writers, including Willie, joined the competition. In the mid-seventies he put together another, more informal team, called the Golden Nematodes, named after a tiny potato bug. Wearing their gold T-shirts, the Nematodes played Sunday afternoons on the field behind Bridgehampton High School. They were a diverse crew, including locals and summer renters, writers and bartenders, adults and teenagers, who, Willie said, were "held together by Jeffersonian democracy and the double steal." David Rae

Roasting pigs at the beach, at the artist Warren Brandt's house in Water Mill.

Morris and Jamie Jones covered the outfield; Willie pitched, played first base, or coached. When he felt well enough, Jim Jones might also take a turn at first.

Bridgehampton was "a village of dogs," Willie wrote about his town, "big country dogs with friendly faces who roam about unencumbered—all honored local personalities." Chief among these was Pete, a middle-aged black Labrador who lived at the service station on Main Street. For his tendency to wander the streets, greeting people, Pete became known as the mayor of Bridgehampton. "Like some kind of modern-day Pied Piper," Kaylie Jones wrote in her memoir, Willie "was a man to whom children and animals were naturally drawn, and they adored him absolutely and blindly." First Pete adopted Willie, and then Willie adopted Pete. "They were kindred spirits," Kaylie remembers. "Wherever [Willie] went, Pete went."

Later, Willie would extol Pete's extraordinary characteristics in the pages of *Reader's Digest*. The Labrador became even more of a local celebrity when an elementary school teacher assigned the article to her students. A few months after that, she invited Willie and Pete to visit her class. In a letter to Omie Parker, Willie's high school teacher, he recalled the event. "I got a friend of mine who owns a long

Willie (center) playing softball for the Golden Nematodes.

black Lincoln Continental limousine to put on a chauffeur's suit and drive us to the school. The children were waiting out front. 'Pete the Mayor' had a bow tie on his collar and was sitting all alone right in the middle of the back seat. My friend opened the back door and said, 'Come along, Your Honor,' and when Pete emerged his chauffeur proceeded to brush him off with a whisk-broom. The kids' eyes were large as saucers."

In January 1976, Willie left Bridgehampton briefly for Washington, D.C. Ed Yoder, who was editorial pages editor of the *Washington Star*, helped Willie secure a spot as a visiting columnist. From January through March, he contributed more than twenty articles, from interviews with politicians and profiles of lounge singers to his account of a road trip that he, Jones, and their boys made to the Jefferson Memorial and Civil War battlefields. "Brilliant daily journalism," Yoder calls Willie's articles, some of which were later collected in the books *Terrains of the Heart* and *Shifting Interludes*.

While in Washington, Willie spent time with a young *Star* reporter named Winston Groom, who was working on his first novel, *Better Times Than These*, about a group of Vietnam War soldiers. Willie and Jones helped edit the book, and Willie sent a letter of introduction to his own agent, Sterling Lord, suggesting that he represent it. Groom codedicated the novel to Jones and later wrote, "Willie is probably the finest line editor in the world." In the 1980s, when Groom finished his quirky novel about an idiot savant, *Forrest Gump*, he sent it first to Willie for his opinion. "He read it and told me, 'Don't change a word! Not one!'" Groom said. Published in 1986, the novel would become a major bestseller after it was made into an Academy Award–winning movie starring Tom Hanks.

On Long Island, in January 1977, Jones's health was deteriorating, and he was hospitalized with congestive heart failure. He was released in February, but during these winter months, Willie's mother also fell sick. The previous December, he had gotten a detailed letter from a neighbor in Yazoo City expressing concern about her. Marion Morris was acting "restless and nervous," the neighbor reported, and among the dozen odd behaviors noted were that she was "falling down on her music as organist" at the First Methodist Church and had recently walked into the Fellowship Hall "minus her shoes." The neighbor went on to question if Mrs. Morris were taking tranquilizers or drinking sherry, and implored Willie to come home immediately. By January, however, Marion was feeling better, and wrote Willie one of her characteristic mother-son letters, exhorting him to "eat correctly—cut down on smoking and drinking."

Then in early April, after suffering a slight stroke, she was admitted to King's Daughters Hospital in Yazoo City. At first she appeared to be recovering, and Willie made a plane reservation to visit in a few days' time. But on April 15, Marion Morris died suddenly, at the age of seventy-two. For more than thirty years, she had been the organist at the First Methodist Church; now at her funeral, Hannah Kelly, wife of Willie's high school coach, played the hymn "Abide with Me." Afterward, Mrs. Morris was buried alongside her husband in Glenwood Cemetery.

Willie stayed in Yazoo City for several weeks after the funeral to clean out his boyhood home and put it up for sale. "The moment came that I stood alone in the empty house. Did I know then how it would grow to haunt my dreams and nightmares? In the gloom of it that day I strained to hear the music again, my father's footsteps on the porch, the echoes of boys playing basketball in the back yard, the barks and whines of Tony, Sam, Jimbo, Sonny, Duke, and Old Skip. I locked the front door and did not look behind me."

During the drive back to Long Island, in his mother's car, Willie spoke to Gloria Jones and learned that Jim had been hospitalized again. Arriving on a Thursday, he went directly to the hospital in Southampton. When the friends saw each other, Jones spoke to Willie again about his finishing *Whistle*, as he'd done on other occasions, and he dictated yet more details for the novel's ending into a tape recorder. He died the following Monday, May 9. In a short time, Willie had lost the people who had been, he felt, the "two great presences in my whole life." After the funeral, he went into the attic of his friend's house, where much of *Whistle* had been written, and organized the tape recordings and notes, a task he undertook as "a sacred duty," Kaylie remembers. In only a few weeks, he had a detailed summary of the last three and a half chapters. When the novel was published the following year, the *New York Times* reviewer noted, "One can scarcely tell where the original text ends and the synopsis begins."

By January 1978, Willie had finished a manuscript about his friendship with Jones, which he hoped would also explain "something about writing, especially about being a writer in America." That month he signed a contract with Doubleday, and Stewart "Sandy" Richardson, the editor-in-chief, suggested a few changes to the draft. At Richardson's urging, Willie contacted several prominent writers and editors who had known Jim Jones—among them Kurt Vonnegut, Burroughs Mitchell, and Irwin Shaw—and asked them to share their reminiscences. The *Atlantic Monthly* published an excerpt from the book in June 1978, and *James Jones: A Friendship*, dedicated to Jim's children, Kaylie and Jamie, came out in October. Willie received many letters from readers who were touched by his depiction of their friendship; in its review, the *New York Times* was more laudatory than it had been for *A Southern Album*. "[It] is as much an autobiography as it is a portrait of another," Christopher Lehmann-Haupt wrote, "and, as self-exploration, it stands as a fitting embellishment to Mr. Morris's earlier autobiographical 'North Towards [sic] Home.'" The *Times* chose the memoir as one of the best books of the year.

Following this success, Sandy Richardson and his staff were enthusiastic about the novels-in-progress that Willie described to them. In November, Willie received a letter from the Sterling Lord

Willie in 1979, as his years in Bridgehampton came to a close.

Agency. "Here is your copy of the fully-executed Doubleday contract for *Taps* and *Chimes at Midnight*. They sure do make a pretty package of their contracts—looks like a Christmas card."

"The death of the last of one's parents is one of life's great divides," Willie wrote in *James Jones: A Friendship*. At age forty-two, he had crossed that milestone. In the fall he wrote to Omie Parker, express-ing the deep grief that he held for his mother. He was also missing home. "The only way this pain is assuaged," he told her, "is by writing about it." He was hard at work on *Taps*, and his work was beginning to "click" in a way it never had. "I hope to finish within a year and . . . I think [it] may be the best writing I've ever done." He concluded by confiding to his mentor, "I feel I have some great books in me that are aching to come out." He would spend the next decade of his life struggling to bring them forth.

SEVEN

"Coming Back to Where His Strongest Feelings Lay"

―――❦―――

Everything that matters in life is hard.
Being a writer not only softens the inevitable pain, but makes it matter.
—Letter from Willie Morris to his student Karen Hinton

THIS TIME, WILLIE'S LIFE-CHANGING CROSS-COUNTRY JOURNEY began not by bus, but in his mother's white '74 Plymouth Valiant, still bearing the Yazoo County license plates. On the wintry morning of January 3, 1980, Willie, accompanied by David Rae and Pete the dog, set out from Bridgehampton and drove as far as Roanoke, Virginia. The next morning it was snowing, so they left early to make another long drive to Dickson, Tennessee, just outside Nashville. On the third day, January 5, they arrived in Oxford, Mississippi. After nearly twenty-eight years, Willie Morris had come home. He was forty-five years old.

Since his mother's death in April 1977, the idea of returning home had been much on Willie's mind. "As if in a dream," he wrote, "where every gesture is attenuated, it grew upon me that a man had best be coming back to where his strongest feelings lay." In July 1977, he had gone to Yazoo City to report for *Time* magazine on President Jimmy Carter's visit there. In an interview the following spring, he'd commented, "It looks like I'm coming down more and more. I'd like to spend more time here."

Then in fall 1978 he had traveled to Hattiesburg, Mississippi, for a speaking engagement, where he'd visited with Larry Wells and his wife, Dean Faulkner Wells, William Faulkner's niece. The

Wellses were owners of a small publishing company in Oxford called Yoknapatawpha Press, named for the fictional Mississippi county where Faulkner had set his books. In Hattiesburg, Wells and Willie had discussed a possible position at the University of Mississippi. By the following spring, Wells and Evans Harrington, chairman of the English Department, were assembling the funds for Willie to become writer-in-residence on campus, where he would give classes in creative writing and the American novel. Willie found himself full of "odd hesitations" about returning to Mississippi, but that fall after visiting the campus for a spirited weekend of tailgating and football, he decided to accept the post.

In many ways, the Mississippi that Willie came back to in 1980 was different from the state that he had left in 1952. The public schools had been integrated for ten years, and Mississippi led the nation in African American officeholders. William Winter, a political moderate who that January was inaugurated as governor, advocated for racial reconciliation and educational reform. In 1962, there had been deadly rioting at the University of Mississippi when James Meredith integrated the campus, but by the mid-1970s the university was recruiting African American students.

Up until the 1970s, Oxford was a quiet college town, not much altered since 1950, when William Faulkner was awarded the Nobel Prize. The courthouse still dominated the square, where the principal businesses included four drugstores, two hardware stores, two dry cleaners, and a sole restaurant. But in the late seventies Oxford became more lively and sophisticated. In an old cotton warehouse, Ron Shapiro started the Hoka Theatre, a revival movie house and café; Richard and Lisa Howorth founded an independent bookstore overlooking the square, in fall 1979; and that same year, William Ferris was appointed the first full-time director of the Center for the Study of Southern Culture. Then Willie Morris arrived.

Willie was pleased to live in Faulkner's hometown and to feel the great writer's spirit, and he would often visit Faulkner's antebellum home, Rowan Oak, and his grave in St. Peter's Cemetery. He was content being back in Mississippi. Whenever he crossed the state line, he said in an interview, his "nerve ends" would "come alive." In May of that year, 1980, Willie sketched his impressions of home for *Inside Sports:*

I like the way they sell chicken and pit-barbecue and fried catfish in
the little stores next to the service stations. I like the way the coeds
make themselves up for their classes. I like the way strangers on the
Square or the Levy's Jitney Jungle finish your sentences for you. I
like the unflagging courtesy of the young, the way they say "Sir" and
"Ma'am." I like the way the white and black people banter with each
other, the old graying black men whiling away their time sitting on
the brick wall in front of the jailhouse, some of them wearing Rebel
baseball caps. I like the intertwining of old family names. I like the
way people remember their dead.

Willie and Pete settled into a rented house at 16 Faculty Row,
a wooden bungalow tucked into the side of a hill. The university-
owned house was sparingly furnished, but there was a fireplace in the
living room and a worktable with a single chair in the dining room
where he would write. On days he didn't teach, Willie would get up
around noon, walk Pete, and then put in several hours at his desk. In
the evenings, he might socialize with friends at the Holiday Inn bar,
stop for dinner at the Sizzler or the Warehouse, make a late visit to
the Hoka, and even later invite a group back to his house. A writer's
life can be lonely, and especially at night, friends recall, Willie didn't
enjoy being alone. "Willie liked to tell stories, and he liked to hear
other people's stories," Richard Howorth remembers.

In Oxford, besides university professors and students, Willie be-
friended a variety of people, from the mayor and state legislator, to in-
surance salesmen and appliance storeowners, to an African American
Vietnam vet and a visiting Japanese scholar. He also became friendly
with Ole Miss coaches and loved attending university baseball, basketball, and football games. Willie was a founding member of "the
South End Zone Rowdies," thirty or so faithful who congregated
there in part because the tickets were cheaper, in part because it was
a laid-back place to watch the game, and in part because they appreciated the company. Among others, the Rowdies included Richard
Howorth and the Wellses, David Sansing and Ron Borne, both professors at the university, Ron Shapiro and Jim Dees from the Hoka,
attorney Semmes Luckett, and novelist Barry Hannah and his wife,
Susan. Willie also belonged to another eclectic group that called
themselves the "Six Horsemen of Clear Creek," who met monthly

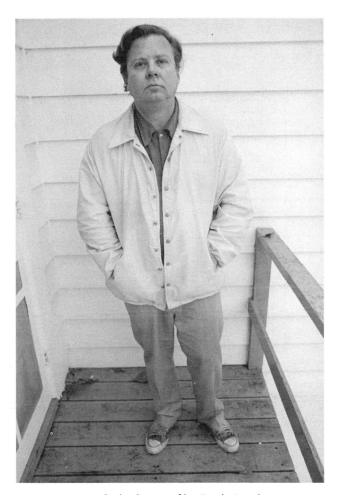

Posing on the back steps of his Faculty Row house.

at a local cabin to grill chicken and steaks and engage in heady conversation ranging from university athletics to Willie's ideas for new books. "Graveyard talk," says Ron Borne. "Whatever we talked about there, stayed out there."

For Willie's twice-weekly class in the American novel, the university selected "seventy-five of the best students." Willie would arrive at the auditorium in Bishop Hall in his usual attire, khakis and a golf shirt, accompanied by the ever-faithful Pete, who would stretch out on the dais. (Willie joked that the Yankee transplant was fast becoming a southerner—learning to eat catfish, collard greens, and ham

Willie, with Pete, in his home office on Faculty Row. He bought his desk at
Cedar Bucket Furniture Company.

hocks.) Willie would assign a dozen and a half books to his students
to read over the course of a semester, including novels by Faulkner,
John Knowles, James Jones, James Dickey, Winston Groom, and
William Styron. Teaching from the perspective of a working writer,
Willie shared his insights into how an author might craft a story, for
example, why he might make a particular choice at a specific point
in the narrative. And there was this bonus: Willie's students had the
opportunity to spend time with many of the writers they were reading, because he invited them, his friends, to be guest lecturers. Then
his classes would be standing room only. But it wasn't only celebrated
writers such as Knowles, Dickey, Plimpton, Groom, and Styron who
turned up at Willie's classes. Motee Daniels, Faulkner's bootlegger,
came, too.

To earn one of the dozen spots in Willie's creative writing class,
students had to submit a sample of their work to a committee for
approval. In their sessions, the students critiqued each other's writing, and Willie would gently weigh in as well. But stressing the im-
portance of reading, he also brought in exemplary short stories and
books to discuss. "He would put emphasis on what the writer was
trying to capture, what emotion," recalls a student, Karen Hinton.

"The class was a mix of craft but also the heart behind the writing." Willie listened intently to what his students said, and remembered their comments from class. "I think that was one of the reasons students really loved him," Karen believes, "not only valued him as a teacher, but loved him as a person."

In Oxford, where he had the services of a secretary, Willie began drafting his manuscripts in longhand, usually with a black felt-tip pen, rather than on a typewriter. He used a system of three-by-five notecards to plan his books. He would record a thought on each card, sometimes paper-clipping an article from his research, and toss the cards into a box. When he was ready to write, he would sort the cards in neat piles on his worktable, and these would become his chapters. "When you got past the top of the table," comments Sid Salter, a friend and fellow writer, "organization was not a word typically used in the same sentence with Willie Morris. But on top of that table, he agonized over words, phrases, [and] really complex linkages that he would draw. He would continue to shuffle those cards both literally and figuratively until he got the order he wanted."

Willie had been working on *Taps* before coming to the university, and he would return to the novel throughout the next decade. Says friend Jim Dees, "*Taps* was this haunting story that hung over him the whole time he was in Oxford." As a protection against fire, Willie took to keeping the manuscript in his freezer. And there was that other novel, *The Chimes at Midnight*, which was set in that other Oxford, in England, which he was still under contract to write for Doubleday. During these years, Willie also began publishing books with Yoknapatawpha Press, including a paperback edition of *North Toward Home*, with an introduction by Ed Yoder, and a new edition of *Good Old Boy*, which he dedicated to his teacher Omie Parker. He later wrote to her: "I was only a kid but you taught me how to write: you taught me the meaning of *words*, and the beauty and efficacy of them. I'm forever in your debt for this immeasurable lesson. You were the best teacher of writing in my life."

In the early eighties, Willie published more in magazines, in part because he needed the added income. The university furnished him only a modest salary, and among the bills to pay was David Rae's tuition at Hampshire College in Amherst, Massachusetts. "Coming on Back" appeared in *Life* in June 1981, and the article moved William

Styron to write Willie, "Your Mississippi piece is absolutely splendid—so tellingly right about the place, so funny, wry, sad and beautiful." It became the opener for a collection brought out in the fall of 1981 by Yoknapatawpha and titled *Terrains of the Heart and Other Essays on Home*.

When Willie became acquainted with an African American high school student from Philadelphia, Mississippi, named Marcus Dupree, the idea for a serious work of nonfiction began to take shape. Dupree was a supremely talented running back who would become the most-sought-after college recruit in the nation. His story appealed to Willie not only because of Marcus's precocious talent, but also because he'd grown up in Neshoba County, where the three young civil rights workers James Earl Chaney, Andrew Goodman, and Michael Schwerner had been murdered during the Freedom Summer of 1964. The book would be an opportunity to weave these disparate stories together, show how sports could be an engine for racial progress, and even reflect on Willie's personal homecoming. His agent, Sterling Lord, was enthusiastic; David Halberstam, who had initially suggested that Willie consider a magazine article on Dupree, was also very encouraging. "It's a book right up your alley," he wrote Willie, "all the things you love and care about. I have Halberstam's Law, which is that the most important thing in a book is the *impulse* behind it—and the degree of impulse, and that's a great index for you on this one."

Since 1980, Willie's publisher Doubleday had been experiencing some disruption in their editorial department. His editor, Sandy Richardson, had been let go, but Willie decided to continue with the venerable house. In September 1980 the new editor-in-chief, Betty Prashker, wrote Willie that she appreciated his "devotion to Doubleday" and let him know that his editor would be Carolyn Blakemore. In July 1981, Willie signed a contract for the Dupree book that, due to the timeliness of the subject, stipulated a manuscript due date of one year later. To make this tight schedule possible, Doubleday agreed to delay his deadlines on *Taps* to January 1983 and *Chimes* to January 1984. That fall Lord wrote Willie to tell him that Herman Gollob, a colleague from *Harper's* days who was now a senior editor at Simon & Schuster, had also expressed interest in publishing him. But still Willie remained loyal to Doubleday.

That same fall, Willie transferred to the university's Department of Journalism, where he taught a magazine seminar and advised the start-up publication the *Ole Miss Magazine*. Limited to a dozen students, the seminar met in Farley Hall to discuss article ideas and production issues, though occasionally they might gather in Willie's favorite restaurant, the Warehouse, where he would entertain them with his stories. "He was an incredible teacher," a student, Anne Glover, recalls. "He didn't accept trite writing." Will Norton, chair of the department, also found Willie to be a great teacher and editor. "He knew a good story," he says, "and he knew whom to assign to each story. So he brought out the best writing in each student. Many of his Ole Miss students have become outstanding writers and reporters. He knew how he wanted each piece written, and he worked with each writer to craft each article." But Willie was commuting nearly 150 miles between Oxford and Philadelphia to research his new book, and sponsoring the magazine cut into his writing; after four issues it folded. Around this time, a friend from the Hamptons wrote him, "The potato field next to your old house wasn't planted this year. It has grown over with weeds . . . I know you won't be back."

The following May, David Rae graduated from Hampshire College. Willie, who was consumed by the Dupree manuscript, didn't attend the ceremony. He wrote his son, "As I said on the phone, I'd like to be with you at your graduation. But your mom will be there giving the commencement speech, and quite frankly I'm very proud of both of you for that." In Mississippi, Marcus Dupree was also graduating, from high school, and he had decided to attend the University of Oklahoma to play for the Sooners.

But the summer of '82 went by without Willie delivering the manuscript to Doubleday. In October, Blakemore wrote his agent: "I'm really getting concerned. . . . The subject seems to me to be increasingly perishable as time passes." The book was turning out to be a huge undertaking, and perhaps a year hadn't been a realistic schedule to complete it. As of January, Willie had secluded himself in a friend's cabin near Oxford. Then while he was finishing up, Pete died, a painful and symbolic loss that Willie described in the book's closing paragraphs. "Something of me was gone with Pete, so much of my deluded youth and vanity, my loves and fears as a writing man, my American comings and goings." Befitting the former

Willie with Pete on one of their many driving trips. Note the Ole Miss T-shirt on the car's front seat.

"mayor of Bridgehampton," Pete's obituary appeared in *Newsday* and the *Southampton Press* on Long Island, but as a resettled southerner, he was buried near St. Peter's Cemetery in Oxford.

By May, Blakemore had Willie's manuscript for the book, which had grown to nearly five hundred typeset pages. Doubleday rushed production to bring it out in the fall of 1983, when they made a major publicity push. They sent Willie on tour; the Literary Guild chose the book as a featured alternate; there was much print and TV coverage; and ads ran in key publications, featuring blurbs by influential writers such as Walker Percy, who called it "the story of a transformation of a town and perhaps a nation by, of all things, sports."

But struggling with injury and a falling out with his coach, Dupree left Oklahoma in October of his sophomore year, just as copies of Willie's book were hitting bookstore shelves and reviewers' desks. Sales were disappointing and reviews mixed, with some complaining that the book was too long, sentimental, and poorly organized, and others extolling it as absorbing, insightful, and well researched. Willie was let down by the uneven reception. Yet the following January, *Marcus Dupree* won a Christopher, an award that had been founded in 1949 to recognize films and books that "affirm the highest values of the human spirit."

Shortly after the publication of *Marcus Dupree*, Yoknapatawpha Press brought out Willie's *Always Stand In Against the Curve*, a collection of six sports essays and a short story, "The Fumble." But he wouldn't publish another book for six years. He continued in the Department of Journalism, in early 1984 receiving a letter of praise from Will Norton: "You have helped us recruit. You have helped raised scholarship monies. You have attracted national attention to the department, but most of all, Willie, you have continued to inspire students to excellence in writing." He was turning out work for magazines, such as *Parade* and *Reader's Digest*. He confessed in a letter to Karen Hinton, "I've been writing magazine pieces merely to accumulate money to pay off old debts and to get back down to my book *Taps*, which is my real baby."

Willie did get back to *Taps*, but for the next few years the novel bedeviled him. By 1987, he was focusing on it intensely, and at the Doubleday offices Carolyn Blakemore was eagerly awaiting the manuscript, which was now called *Echoes*. In early spring of 1988, Willie was in seclusion near McComb, Mississippi, on the Bogue Chitto River, and still writing. The university was supportive, and encouraged him to take whatever time he needed to finish the novel. By this point, he had shed his teaching responsibilities in the Journalism Department, although he continued as writer-in-residence and still invited friends and former colleagues to lecture, including *Harper's* contributors David Halberstam, Larry L. King, and Marshall Frady, and the Mississippi writers Ellen Gilchrist and Beth Henley.

But *Taps* wasn't the only project Willie had under way. That spring, he got a letter from JoAnne Prichard, a beautiful and creative senior editor at the University Press of Mississippi. Just as in Bridgehampton, in Oxford it was often hard to reach Willie by phone. In the mid-seventies, Willie had started using a telephone code involving a fixed number of rings, to let him know that a friend was calling; he changed the code from time to time as it was "leaked." As a result, many people resorted to writing him. In her letter to Willie, JoAnne told him about a new series from the University Press that paired Mississippi writers and artists, and invited him to

Willie in front of William Faulkner's house, Rowan Oak.
He often visited the historic home and walked the grounds.

contribute essays for the second volume, which would be illustrated by the painter William Dunlap.

Willie had known JoAnne since the 1960s, when she was a teacher in the Yazoo City public schools; in 1976, he had written an introduction to a book that she had coauthored, *Yazoo: Its Legends and Legacies*. Now when she didn't hear back from him about her publishing proposal, she wrote their mutual friend David Sansing. He suggested that on a certain day and at a specific hour she stand at the back steps of the journalism building and meet Willie as he was coming out the door. The plan worked, and he and his soon-to-be editor repaired to the Holiday Inn bar to hammer out the details for the book, to be called *Homecomings*.

Meanwhile at Doubleday, there was yet more change in the editorial department. Carolyn Blakemore was asked to resign and Willie's former colleague Herman Gollob was hired as editor-in-chief. In early June, he wrote Willie that he expected *Echoes* within the month or he would "start hollering." Willie sent the manuscript, and on August 4, Gollob delivered bad news. "Why, as the feller said," he began, "you're a writin' fool. . . . This doesn't mean the novel is ready to be sent to the printer. You have miles to go before you sleep, old buddy. But the important thing is, the end is in sight, and getting there's going to be fun."

He went on to give Willie numerous editorial suggestions, along with those of a talented young editor, Shaye Areheart. She had concluded that "without a doubt" the manuscript was publishable, and believed that with some rewriting, it might become a bestseller. One of the changes she recommended was reverting the book's title to *Taps*. Sterling Lord was also an admirer of the manuscript. "I know Herman has sent you a revision letter," he wrote Willie, "but the overriding factor is that your writing is beautiful and it's a pleasure to be reading you again."

Doubleday's insistence on so many alterations to the novel that Willie had been writing for so long, and that meant so much to him, came as a blow. But he considered their comments carefully, and by early October Areheart had his reply. They were in sync about cutting some scenes, moving and rewriting some chapters, and sharpening the relationships among the characters. "I was so happy to get your letter and hear that you thought some of my ideas were helpful that I walked around with a smile on my face for about a week," Areheart wrote him. With her encouragement, Willie went back to *Taps* with new energy.

At the end of 1988, JoAnne Prichard wrote to Willie, thanking him for contributing six essays to *Homecomings*. "I hope your work on *Taps* is productive," she said, "and that life in general is great in '89." In May, he finished revising the novel; Sterling Lord, believing it substantially improved, sent it back to Gollob. But Gollob decided that *Taps* wasn't publishable, and Willie was devastated. "We wanted

Willie with good friend Bill Ferris, director of the Center for the Study of Southern
Culture, on the porch at Square Books, 1990.

a plot-driven novel," Gollob was later quoted as saying. "Willie wanted more of a lyrical, episodic book." Lord rushed the manuscript to
three other New York firms, two of which rejected it. Willie with-
drew the third submission, choosing to rework *Taps* yet again.

Willie continued struggling with financial pressures, including
back taxes. In May, he got a long, loving letter from David Rae, outlining his concerns over his father's drinking, which had intensified
during his years in Bridgehampton and Oxford. Some of Willie's
friends were also worried, David wrote. But Willie justified his de-
pendence on alcohol by pointing out that many respected writers
drank, at times excessively, and he believed his own drinking to be in
that tradition. Although they remained in touch, Willie and David
Rae's relationship was strained for a time. Willie was also smoking
heavily, the Viceroys that his mother had warned him about.

But there was also a welcome development in his life. By mid-
1989, he had begun a romance with JoAnne Prichard. That fall, she
would drive to Oxford from her home in Jackson to attend football
games with Willie and his friends. Now and again, she and Willie
would meet at Greenville's landmark steakhouse, Doe's Eat Place.
Willie started spending time in Jackson, staying downtown in the

Willie signing *Faulkner's Mississippi* at Square Books.

Sun-n-Sand Motor Hotel, where he worked on the manuscript for *Faulkner's Mississippi*. In March of that year, *National Geographic* had printed Willie's long article by that title, which he was revising for a lavish book, with photography by William Eggleston, to be issued by Oxmoor House in fall 1990. But first, two other books of Willie's would appear in the fall of 1989—the sequel *Good Old Boy and the Witch of Yazoo*, published by Yoknapatawpha, and *Homecomings*, which would win the Authors Award for nonfiction from the Mississippi Library Association.

In May 1990, Mississippi senator Thad Cochran threw a grand party in Washington, D.C., for the twentieth anniversary of the University Press and for *Homecomings*. JoAnne and Willie drove up for the gala. There, from the podium in the august Senate Caucus Room, Willie quipped that he liked JoAnne's editing so much that he wanted to marry her. Many in the crowd wondered whether he was serious, but she knew. And so the couple became engaged. In his inscription to her on the title page of *Faulkner's Mississippi*, he would later write: "To my dearest JoAnne, who reminded me again of love."

During Willie's years in Oxford, he had reveled in being back in his home state, where, after the reversal at *Harper's* and his self-exile on Long Island, he had gone to reinvent himself. But at times he had struggled with loneliness and downheartedness, with his finances and drinking, and with his work. At the university, he had mentored a decade of journalists and fiction writers, including Steve Yarbrough, Donna Tartt, and John Grisham, and he had helped convert the college town of Oxford into a magnet for literature. By his presence at the university and through his writings, he had burnished the reputation of the institution, which had still been suffering from its role in the James Meredith crisis. Willie Morris was poised to enter one of the most fruitful and satisfying decades of his life.

EIGHT

"Bittersweet, but Fine"

Finding Serenity in Jackson

———— ⊂•⊃ ————

> At age 59, going on 60, I've never been happier or more serene. This is 100%
> because of JoAnne. Her extraordinary kindness, beauty, and brains saved
> my life. . . . And she isn't even conscious of the happiness she elicits in me.
> Well, maybe she is. She's from Indianola, after all. It's this late happiness that
> makes *me* so happy, and sad. Happiness is bittersweet, but fine.
> —*Willie Morris, "Memo to Myself," dated September 24, 1994, and discovered
> posthumously among his letters*

ON SEPTEMBER 14, 1990, A VERY WARM AND SUNNY DAY, WILLIE
Morris and JoAnne Prichard married in the late afternoon on the
back deck of her house in Jackson. Only their immediate families were present, and David Rae stood for his father as best man.
That evening, they held a reception downtown at Hal & Mal's, a
self-described "upscale honky-tonk" co-owned by brothers Hal and
Malcolm White. In the restaurant courtyard, potted trees were placed
on tables to create a canopy of green, and votive candles were hid-
den in the niches of the old brick wall to throw soft, flickering light.
Friends gathered to celebrate with the newlyweds over drinks and
hors d'oeuvres, including Mississippi hot tamales the way Willie liked
them—sliced into rounds and served on saltines. There was wedding
cake to cut, and rhythm-and-blues played by some members of the
Tangents.

The next day, Saturday, the couple attended the Ole Miss–Auburn
football game in Jackson and afterward drove the forty miles north
to Yazoo City. They ate dinner in the unassuming Steak House

Willie and JoAnne on the day of their marriage, September 14, 1990.

restaurant and spent the night in the equally unassuming Yazoo Motel, a low-slung brick building at the intersection of highways 49 East and West, known as Four Points. "The most underrated motel in America" was how Willie described the lodgings, which had been built in the 1950s to resemble a Holiday Inn.

After this brief honeymoon, Willie moved permanently to Jackson. He had come full circle to the place of his birth, where as a boy he had spent many happy days visiting his maternal grand-parents and great-aunts. The largest city in the state, Jackson had become a sprawling, modern capital, but Willie was still a public person there, as he had been in the much smaller town of Oxford. On his return, he was proud of both the Jackson of his memory and the city he experienced in his day-to-day life, and he inspired others to be proud. He invited many of his out-of-town friends to visit and get to know the capital, showing them, as Malcolm White recalls, "that this is a good place, with good people." Willie took his friends to meet the mayor and the governor, because as a kind of ambassador, he had carte blanche wherever he went. Whether his visitors were from New York or Hollywood, Austin, Texas, or Oxford, England, he wanted to connect them to Mississippi and to connect the state

William Styron visiting Willie and JoAnne at their home in
Jackson not long after their wedding.

to the wider world. "He was the Pied Piper," White says, "the cultural
czar of Mississippi."

Despite his public persona, Willie was able to be more anonymous
in the larger city, his life more private. He settled into JoAnne's small
house on the corner of Northside Drive and Normandy. Often he
would leave little notes around the house for her to find, letting her
know what a wonderful wife she was. In *My Cat Spit McGee*, Willie
would describe how, as an inveterate dog man, he came to love a
cat, but really the book was about how his life was transformed by
JoAnne. He would write of her: "She was a Delta girl, and I a Delta
boy. Somehow she could change personae, swift as April rainfalls:
one day she might look like a schoolteacher, the next a beauty queen,
then an unabashed doyenne of the cognoscenti."

They cared for the same things—"lingering landscapes and memories," the call of the mockingbird and the sight of the new moon,
Christmases at home with a fine cedar tree and all the family gathered. He lauded her talents, often telling friends, "She's the best editor in the South." She became first reader of his manuscripts; they

would sign their notes "The Writer" and "The Editor." Over time they acquired other nicknames for each another, with Willie called "WillieMo" or "Mo" and JoAnne "JAM," or "Jambone," or "BOI," for "Belle of Indianola." Occasionally, a friend might address a letter to them both as "MOJO," as if they were one person. While Willie derived serenity from the marriage, Joanne felt excitement because "life was a lot more interesting. . . . I know that Willie brought the best out in me, and I think I brought out the best in him," she says. "It was a case of two plus two equals five."

They established a relaxed domestic routine. Willie was fond of inviting good friends, such as Peyton Prospere and Rick and Liz Cleveland and their children Annie and Tyler, over to dinner, and on occasion he would cook. He had two or three easy dishes that he liked to prepare, including spaghetti. Or, always the practical joker, he might buy some ribs and brag that he had barbecued them himself. Once he got ambitious and baked a goose, but when the bird came from the oven the meat was so shrunken that there weren't two bites apiece for the guests, and everybody had a laugh.

These were good times, and there was often laughter. He and JoAnne would also eat out with friends, in downhome Jackson standbys such as the Mayflower Cafe, Crechale's, or Bill's Burger House. Hal & Mal's was another favorite, where the public Willie would hold court from a big round table in the corner. He spent so much time there, remembers Malcolm White, that the restaurant installed a phone jack for his use. Very often, parents would come over to thank him for writing *Good Old Boy*, telling him how much their son or daughter had enjoyed the book. If the child happened to be present, he or she would invariably ask, "Is everything in there true?" And this would be Willie's cue to give his standard response, with a wink to Mark Twain: "Sometimes you have to lie to tell the truth."

But as much as Willie liked socializing with friends, he loved having family home, especially during the holidays. He had been an only child, but now he presided over a large extended family. At Thanksgivings and Christmases, David Rae would visit with his partner, Susanne Dietzel; JoAnne's sons, Gibson and Graham, would also come with their girlfriends and wives, along with her brother, Jay Shirley, and his wife. At the table would often be close friend Ron Shapiro, from Oxford. For these dinners, Willie would write out

Willie and JoAnne holding court at Hal & Mal's. Willie frequented the restaurant so often they installed his own phone jack.

elaborate menus, in felt tip on white poster paper, incorporating the names of the guests and Mississippi place names. (One Christmas menu included "Fresh Scottish Smoked Salmon Indianola," "Willie's Christmas Surprise Yazoo," and "Ineluctable Indian Corn Pudding Pocahontas.") JoAnne recalls, "Willie liked to play, and he gave play as much seriousness as he gave writing."

During these years, he was finally putting his financial problems behind him, and he was drinking less. With happiness and more structure at home came greater productivity. As usual, Willie wrote in the afternoons. JoAnne would be at her job at the University Press offices, and he experienced few interruptions. In fact, during the next decade he would publish almost as many books as he had in all the prior years combined.

Willie resigned as writer-in-residence at the University of Mississippi in February 1991. A month later, he sent Sterling Lord a proposal for a sequel to *North Toward Home*, a memoir about the sixties and his editorship of *Harper's*. He knew the book would be a major work, and he wrote his agent, "How about our taking bids on this? . . . I really want to get the most lucrative contract possible on *New York Days*, and I honestly think it deserves one." Lord agreed and sent to publishers, along with Willie's proposal, copies of his first book and a reflective and poignant article he'd published in *Esquire* about his divorce from Celia. Their story would need to be part of anything that Willie might write about that decade, and happily, when the article had appeared in June 1990, it had served as a balm between them, moving Celia to thank Willie and wish him well in his new marriage.

After sending off the proposal, Willie embarked with JoAnne on an all-expenses-paid trip to Oxford, England, a sort of delayed honeymoon and business trip. He hadn't been to Oxford in more than two decades, and *American Way* magazine had assigned him to write about the visit. Back in New York, Sterling Lord successfully auctioned *New York Days*, earning a $100,000 advance. After he got home from England, Willie confronted the demanding project. There was a basement room in the Northside Drive house that he called "the Dungeon," which became his study. He would quip that JoAnne "did not exactly lock me in, but it felt like it." In reality, Willie went of his own accord into the Dungeon, for five or six hours a day. He had thought about the sequel for a long time, JoAnne says, but "I think only after we were married did he feel comfortable going back into his past, into bad times as well as good." She provided encouragement, and as he wrote they discussed his progress, on the deck in the late afternoons.

As part of his preparation for the book, Willie solicited memories from many of the writers he'd published in *Harper's*—Gay Talese, Edwin Shrake, Larry L. King, and David Halberstam, among others. But to conjure the sixties fully, he needed to do substantial research on the history and politics of the period. To find the reference works he needed, he asked his friend John Evans, owner of Lemuria, an independent bookstore in Jackson, to hunt the out-of-print market. As he had in Oxford at Square Books, Willie became a close friend to the staff at Lemuria, and they, too, followed his writing progress.

That progress was swift. By Christmas 1991, Fredrica Friedman, Willie's editor at the Boston publisher Little, Brown, had a draft of the first half of *New York Days*. While Willie was finishing the manuscript, during 1992, two other books of his came out—*My Two Oxfords*, a previously published essay (in *Homecomings*) that compared his experience of Oxford, England, with that of Oxford, Mississippi; and *After All, It's Only a Game*, a collection of sports essays paired with the fantastical paintings of Jackson artist Lynn Green Root. By February 1993, Friedman had the entire manuscript of *New York Days*, revised and ready for production. Willie codedicated the memoir to his managing editor at *Harper's*, Bob Kotlowitz, and to JoAnne, "Who wasn't there, but should have been."

When *New York Days* launched in August 1993, more than thirty periodicals weighed in with reviews. As is often the case in publishing, opinions varied, depending on the taste of the critic. The book was either "an especially beautiful piece of writing" or a specimen of "purple prose"; a "vivid sequel" to *North Toward Home* or "occasionally oblique"; abounding in "name-dropping" or supplying "little good stuff." But the industry's gold standard, the Sunday *New York Times Book Review*, gave over its entire front page to *New York Days*, complete with a color photo of Willie. The long, appreciative essay by novelist Elizabeth Hardwick recapitulated the events at *Harper's* from Willie's viewpoint.

But Hardwick's review prompted a backlash in the pages of the *Times*. Lewis Lapham was a *Harper's* contributing editor who had been hired after the others and hadn't resigned along with them in 1971; several years later, he had become the magazine's editor-in-chief. Now he wrote a letter to the editor with his version of events, along with a stinging critique of Willie's book, which he found to be overly sentimental. William Blair, who had been the magazine's president and publisher, also wrote taking exception to Willie's account. Responding that he was "more bemused than aggrieved," Willie rebutted Lapham's rebuttal in the *Times*. More than two decades later, the circumstances of his heated departure from *Harper's* were still provoking controversy.

That fall, Willie and JoAnne attended pub parties for *New York Days*, from Elaine's in Manhattan to Scholz Garten in Austin, and they traveled the country on a promotional tour. The book was excerpted in several publications, including *New York* magazine and the *Washington Post*, and Willie found himself in demand for print, television, and radio interviews. "I'm glad I waited twenty-six years," he commented to journalist Charlie Rose about the sequel's timing. "I needed that passing of time to deal with my own sense of memory. . . . I also had to have settled back happily into my native soil of the Deep South to have been able to write it." David Rae Morris believes that

Willie and JoAnne in front of Elaine's for the publication party of *New York Days* in September 1993.

New York Days was cathartic for his father. "It gave him the chance to go back and reexamine the past and deal with it. . . . And he was free of it." The book went on to win the 1994 nonfiction award from the Mississippi Institute of Arts and Letters. That same year, Willie also received the Governor's Arts Award from the Mississippi Arts Commission for his entire body of work.

The next year Willie and JoAnne moved into a larger, two-story house on nearby Brookdale Street in time to celebrate her fiftieth birthday in March. Willie loved the house, which had been built in 1940 with fireplaces, high ceilings, and a long, sloping backyard; he also loved that former governor William Winter lived across the street, a fact that he bragged about in a country-boy-makes-good kind of way.

Even as Willie had been embroiled with publicity for *New York Days*, he had pondered his next book. At the end of 1993, he had decided to change representation, advising Sterling Lord, "I feel myself very much in the need of a 'hungrier' agent." By spring, he had contracted with Theron Raines, his friend Winston Groom's agent, and they were discussing Willie's next projects, including his unfinished novels, *The Chimes at Midnight* and *Taps*. But Raines suggested that first Willie collect everything he'd written about his childhood dog, Skip, and expand it to book length. JoAnne had the idea that this next memoir could be brief. "I had been saying, you don't always have to write really long books," she recalls, "you could write some short books."

Ever since his days on the *Daily Texan*, Willie had published stories about Skip, and now he quickly worked up a draft manuscript of thirty-five thousand words with, as he wrote to Raines, "an abundance of new material." He sent it to the agent along with a note thanking him for the suggestion; he also urged him to get "top dollar" for the little memoir, and to start setting up a movie deal. Afterward, Willie said that he had enjoyed writing *My Dog Skip* more than any of his other books.

While Raines was shopping the *Skip* manuscript to publishers, Willie turned his attention to his upcoming children's book, *A Prayer for the Opening of the Little League Season*. One day while he had been browsing in Lemuria, John Evans, who was a patron of Little League Baseball, had proposed that Willie write a prayer that could be printed as a poster and sold to raise funds for local teams. When Evans sent Willie's verses to Barry Moser, a friend and well-known illustrator, the idea for a children's book took form.

In New York, one of the editors considering *My Dog Skip* was Bob Loomis at Random House. For a long time Willie had wanted to work with Loomis, Styron's editor, who was considered among the best in publishing. Loomis started reading the manuscript one evening on the subway while on his way home from the office. "I really felt wonderful and moved as I hadn't been in a long time," he immediately wrote Willie. "Please don't let Theron sell this to anyone else." In the end, Loomis did acquire the rights to the book, paying the same six-figure amount that Willie had received for *New York Days*. "This is the beginning of a wonderful friendship," Loomis wrote his new author, evoking the closing lines from one of Willie's favorite movies, *Casablanca*. In October, Raines sent Willie the contract for *My Dog Skip*, with a note saying, "I want this to be one of many. . . . I'm looking to the Random House/Bob Loomis connection to raise you to a new plateau."

But in 1994, something momentous was taking place in Jackson that would occupy Willie for the next few years. At the Hinds County courthouse, Byron De La Beckwith was being retried for the 1963 murder of civil rights leader Medgar Evers. The Greenwood fertilizer salesman and professed white supremacist had already been prosecuted twice for the crime, but the trials had ended with hung juries. After Jackson *Clarion-Ledger* reporter Jerry Mitchell discovered fresh evidence, assistant district attorney Bobby DeLaughter put Beckwith on trial for a third time.

David Rae Morris had been working as a staff photographer for newspapers in Mississippi and Tennessee since the early 1980s, before completing a master's degree in journalism at the University of Minnesota and an internship at the *Los Angeles Times*. He was still living in Minnesota but attending the Beckwith trial in Jackson, and he encouraged his father to join him in the courtroom. Willie became absorbed by the historic drama and wrote about it for a *Reader's Digest* publication. After Beckwith was found guilty, Willie got in touch with a longtime contact, Hollywood producer Fred Zollo, about a possible movie, and then wrote a treatment with Bobby DeLaughter as the protagonist. Rob Reiner agreed to direct the project, which would be called *Ghosts of Mississippi*, and the young boy from Yazoo who'd been so enthralled with the big screen in the Dixie Theater became a consultant to the movie industry. Willie "absolutely loved the movies," JoAnne explains. In fact, she knew when he was gearing himself up to start writing because late at night he would watch his favorites, *Chariots of Fire* and *Hoosiers*.

In November, on the eve of his sixtieth birthday, Willie received a mockup of the cover for *My Dog Skip* from Random House. It moved him to tears, he reported to Loomis: "'That's ol' Skip and me,' I said to myself. 'We were really like that.'" The next day, at Hal & Mal's, Willie was surprised with a "North (Jackson) Toward Home Birthday Dinner." Hundreds gathered to wish him well, from childhood friends in Yazoo to colleagues from New York. Many who were unable to attend sent their good wishes, including President Bill Clinton, who had met Willie many years before, on the eve of his own embarkation to Oxford University. David Rae emceed the roast, which was staged as a mock trial. Willie was "arrested" and "charged" on several counts, including perpetrating "malicious mischief,"

Sheriff Malcolm McMillin (right) reading the charges against a handcuffed Willie during his sixtieth birthday party at Hal & Mal's.

"highfalutin' language," and "excessive and oppressive late night sentimentality." Handcuffed by the Hinds County sheriff, he was found guilty and sentenced by Judge E. Grady Jolly to have "a continuing prodigious memory . . . to see forever the essential goodness in the world . . . never to grow up" and "to be smothered in the love, affection, and mirth of your thousands of fans and friends."

During the spring of 1995, *A Prayer for the Opening of the Little League Season* was published just as the Major League players were ending their acrimonious strike, the longest in the sport's history. Also that spring, *My Dog Skip* came out. As *New York Days* had been a reprise of Willie's literary life in New York, *Skip* was the reprise of his childhood in Yazoo City. Willie toured for both books; often when he was in stores signing *Skip*, readers would bring their dogs. There were promotions to find families for homeless dogs, and canine literary contests with Willie choosing the dogs that most resembled famous writers. Random House had wisely decided to market *My Dog Skip* as a book for adults, and both the hardcover and the later paperback edition sold well. *Skip* was affectionately reviewed by the critics, and as Willie had hoped, movie rights were sold, to producer John Lee Hancock and director Jay Russell.

The following year, Willie became engrossed with the filming of *Ghosts of Mississippi*. As part of his consulting duties, he read the screenplay for historical accuracy and suggested locations throughout the state. Myrlie Evers-Williams, Medgar's widow, was a consultant as well. That May, when the local filming finished, Willie and JoAnne threw the cast and crew a backyard party, the invitation promising a "Southern-Style Dinner on the Grounds and Blues Music."

With his attention on Hollywood, Willie again put off work on his two novels. In addition, another idea had come to him, from old friend George Plimpton. Willie sent off to Loomis a proposal for a new nonfiction book nominally about the making of *Ghosts of Mississippi*, but which would explore "the Hollywood culture" and "racism in today's America." He hoped to finish a first draft within a matter of months. In September, Willie and JoAnne flew to Los Angeles to see the rough cut of *Ghosts*, and that December they attended premieres in New York and four days later, in Jackson. But the movie's box office performance and its critical reception proved disappointing, with many reviewers suggesting that the film should have focused on the life of Medgar Evers more than on the conviction of his killer.

Willie's proposed book took longer to write than he'd planned. *The Ghosts of Medgar Evers: A Tale of Race, Murder, Mississippi, and Hollywood* was published in February 1998, a little over a year after the movie's premiere. Like the movie, the book received mixed reviews, although the *New York Times* selected it as one of the "Notable Books" of that year. After his promotional tour, Willie confessed in a letter to his friend and biographer/bibliographer Jack Bales that he felt "rather depressed," although he added, "this always happens to me when a new book comes out." He and JoAnne planned a short break, a road trip to Louisiana's Cajun Country.

Soon after they got home, filming was about to begin on *My Dog Skip*, which for logistical reasons would be shot primarily in Canton, Mississippi, not Yazoo City. Once more, Willie and JoAnne threw a backyard party, this time to welcome the cast, crew, and media. Again, Willie acted as a consultant for the filmmakers and spent time on the set. He became especially close to the twelve-year-old boy who played him on screen, Frankie Muniz. Kevin Bacon and Diane Lane had the parts of Mr. and Mrs. Morris, and Willie took to introducing the youthful actors as "my parents."

All that spring and summer, he was mulling his unfinished novels. He wrote Shaye Areheart, the former Doubleday editor who had read a draft of *Taps* nearly a decade before. She offered to reread the manuscript and advised him not to cut it drastically, as he was proposing. And she urged him to find a publisher for the book. "You are keeping a classic out of circulation," she wrote. But Willie was about to start two new nonfiction books. In October, he attended a planning meeting in Jackson with Seetha Srinivasan, the director of the University Press, about *My Mississippi*, an oversize book that would marry Willie's text with David Rae's color photographs.

The second book was *My Cat Spit McGee*, about a white kitten, the runt of its litter, which Willie had nursed with an eyedropper and named after the mischievous character in *Good Old Boy*. The idea for the book had been sparked by Bailey Browne, Jill Conner Browne's young daughter. By this time, JoAnne had retired from the University Press and was working as a freelance editor, including acquiring titles for the Crown Publishing Group, a sister company of Willie's publisher Random House. Among the books she found for them was Browne's best-selling *The Sweet Potato Queens' Book of Love*.

One day, when Bailey went with her mother to the house on Brookdale, she and Willie spent half an hour talking in the backyard. When he came inside, he announced, "I'm going to write a book called *My Cat Spit McGee*." When Bailey's own pet died soon after, Willie expressed his condolences in a letter. "You just must remember your 'Boy Cat' as long as you yourself live. In never forgetting him in your own immemorial, indwelling heart, then he will live too. That is where sorrow lives, and love. As you will learn as the years pass, this is life itself, and sorrow ... You *must* hurt because you loved him. His memory will become a part of who you are forever. Keep him in your lovely heart." Willie would dedicate *My Cat Spit McGee* to his young friend.

In December 1998, Willie sent Loomis a sample chapter. "Spit is wonderful," his editor responded. "You're at the top of your form." By the end of January, Loomis had received the remaining manuscript. Random House planned to bring out *Spit McGee* that fall. It would be another small-format memoir, which Willie saw as a sequel to *My Dog Skip*. By April, he was busy researching the Mississippi book, trying to tie up the manuscript by his approaching deadline. All that spring, he and JoAnne took many car trips, so that he could write vividly about his home state. But he confessed to Jack Bales, "Quite frankly I'm a little tired. I just seem to work, work. And the money diminishes all the time, forever and ever. . . . Someday I'll drop dead at my work desk. Could do worse, I guess." In addition to finishing the two new books, Willie was also writing for magazines, including a long piece about Eudora Welty for the May issue of *Vanity Fair*. He had met Miss Welty when he was eight or nine, at the vegetable counter of the Jitney Jungle in Belhaven. He had been with his great-aunt Mag, who had whispered to him as they walked away, "She writes those stories *her own self*."

After Willie had moved to Jackson, he and Miss Welty had cultivated their friendship. He and JoAnne liked taking long drives on the weekends, sometimes to Raymond to visit his family's plot in the cemetery, but especially to Yazoo City. Once they invited Miss Welty along. Willie always followed the same route: down the steep hill of Broadway, out Main Street, back on Washington Street by the Methodist Church and Ricks Library, through Glenwood Cemetery to visit the witch's grave, past Willie's boyhood home on Grand Avenue, and ending overlooking the Delta. This time, they were deep in Yazoo County with Miss Welty riding shotgun, and at the crest of a hill, they came to an intersection. Willie said, "Eudora, I'm going to make a left and drive down Paradise Road." She replied, "We'd be fools if we didn't."

Just before Mother's Day, JoAnne left Jackson for Nashville, to celebrate the first birthday of her grandson Addison. In her luggage, she found this handwritten note from Willie:

Dearest JoAnne,
    You deserve to be very happy on this Mother's Day. And here's why.
    Professionally, you've really come into your own as an editor, nationally now and not just regionally (although that's important, too). I'm warmly proud of you for this, but not in the least surprised. I told you all along. You're a truly *great* editor, and your unerring instincts

derive from your heart. Always respond to your Indianola heart. Always trust your instincts.

Your sons adore you for your fealty and love, and now you have Addison. You're a terrific mother.

Your friends love you because you're loyal, funny, and true.

Your little cats Spitty, Mamie, and Bessie love you because you care for them and are a Cat Woman. You made us all this beautiful, beautiful house.

And your husband loves you because . . . well, because along with my grandma Mamie you're the best person I ever knew. *I love you.* You've helped me so.

Great Mother's Day, Love! WMo

On July 12, Willie finished his draft of *My Mississippi*, initialing and dating the last manuscript page, something he'd never done before. He had also reviewed the copyedited manuscript for *Spit* and had returned it to Random House. And he was in the planning stage of another small memoir. That week, Willie had sent a book proposal to Bob Loomis for "a personal memoir about baseball. It's really about my father and me and our bond in baseball—baseball within the broader context of my life, with my father as a central thread." He was thinking of a manuscript of fifty thousand words, slightly longer than *Skip* and *Spit*, which he would call *One for My Daddy: A Baseball Memory.*

"As I dwell on his story and baseball," he wrote his editor, "I realize in the perspective of the years that he didn't abdicate his responsibility as a parent, that in fact it was my father and our bond in baseball that helped me make the critical decisions in my life: teaching me baseball kept me out from under the total control of my mother; giving me the Smith-Corona typewriter to write about baseball for the town paper really started me out as a writer; and insisting that I leave Mississippi and go to the University of Texas, because they had a great baseball field and team—the Texas years opening up the whole world to me."

Then in late July, Willie and JoAnne traveled to New York for a private advance showing of *My Dog Skip*. Afterward, Willie raved about the movie and stayed up late calling friends, including the director, Jay Russell. They returned to Jackson that Friday, July 30. JoAnne remembers it being a hard trip, and that Willie seemed winded from having to walk so far in the airport. The following Sunday, they went riding. Willie stopped at a convenience store, and when he got back in the car he mentioned that he felt lethargic. He'd never said anything like that before. That night, he called David Rae twice at his home in New Orleans with suggestions for the photographs in the Mississippi book.

The next morning, JoAnne was having a meeting downstairs in her home office, when she heard Willie call her name. She ran upstairs and saw he was still in bed and was having trouble breathing. An ambulance was called. As he lay on the gurney on his way from the house, he told JoAnne, "I've got to get my baseball book done." He and JoAnne said how much they loved each other. But even then, she thought that he would be in the hospital for only a few days, and in her mind she was making a list of things she would have to get together—toothbrush, pajamas. She tried to calm him, but Willie seemed to have a presentiment. He told her not to grieve, but added, "Well, grieve a little." He told her to be happy and fulfilled. And he asked her to "get *Taps* together."

Once in the emergency room at St. Dominic Hospital, Willie wanted JoAnne to invite the medical staff gathered around his gurney to the premiere of *My Dog Skip*. "She's the best wife I ever had!" he told them. But that afternoon, Willie lapsed into unconsciousness. David Rae was called, and started the long drive from New Orleans to Jackson. As word spread about Willie's condition, close friends crowded into his room at the hospital. They held his hand and comforted him, and for a time his color improved and his pulse became stronger. But early that evening, Willie died of heart failure. The date was August 2, 1999.

◆ ◆ ◆

Willie Morris had not lived his life to live for a long time, and at sixty-four, he was gone too soon. After intensive planning, Mississippi buried him in a manner befitting a most treasured son. He lay in state at the Old Capitol, where Mississippi had seceded from the Union; he was the first writer, and only the third person that century, to be accorded the honor. Hundreds filed by his flower-laden coffin in downtown Jackson that stiflingly hot, clear day, August 5.

Willie's funeral at the First United Methodist Church in Yazoo City, August 5, 1999.

The funeral service was held forty miles north, in the late afternoon, at the First United Methodist Church in Yazoo City. Civil rights activist Will D. Campbell gave the opening remarks, then called for a standing ovation in celebration of Willie's life. The Reverend Larry Speed read from the Old and New Testaments. Hannah Kelly, wife of Willie's basketball coach Harold Kelly and inheritor of Marion Morris's seat at the organ bench, played the prelude and interlude to Willie's service. Mississippi vocalist Rhonda Richmond gave a rendition of one of his favorite hymns, "Amazing Grace," and the Methodist Church choir sang "Abide with Me" and "In the Garden."

Eulogies were given by luminaries from Willie's diverse world—the writers William Styron, David Halberstam, and Josephine Ayres Haxton (who wrote under the pen name Ellen Douglas), former congressman Mike Espy, and Willie's algebra teacher at Yazoo High, Harriet DeCell Kuykendall, who read a passage from *North Toward Home* about her student's lifelong fondness for the town's cemetery. Willie's neighbor, ex-governor William Winter, said that for those who grew up "in a Mississippi of myths and legends, of fantasy about what never was and hope for what might never be, of insufferable baseness and incredible goodness, he was the one who perhaps more than anybody else of our generation caused us to look within ourselves and discover there the joy and inspiration to sustain us through the good times and the bad."

At the graveside service, in Glenwood Cemetery, a trio of musicians performed "Darkness on the Delta," "Brokedown Palace," and "We'll Meet Again." Jill Conner Browne and Winston Groom gave brief remarks. Will Campbell offered the committal from the *Book of Common Prayer*, "Taps" was sounded, with its echo, and Willie's body was entrusted to the earth.

And so Willie Morris returned to the town of his boyhood and adolescence, the town that had inspired his memories and his writing. In time, his tombstone would be placed thirteen steps from the heavy chain links of the witch's grave, in the historic part of Glenwood. The tombstone would be carved in Austin, Texas, from lovely gray schist, the same rock that had formed New York City. And the words carried on the stone would be, "Even across the divide of death, friendship remains an echo forever in the heart."

Epilogue

———————❦———————

ALL THAT AUGUST, AFTER WILLIE DIED, MANY DOZENS OF OBIT-
uaries ran in publications across the country, from the *New York
Times* to the *Scott County* (Mississippi) *Times*, from the *Washington
Post* to the *Austin American-Statesman*. In appreciation of their native
son, both the Jackson *Clarion-Ledger* and the *Yazoo Herald* published
numerous articles about Willie in the days and weeks following his
death. *Time* magazine printed a tribute from sitting president Bill
Clinton, who wrote, "He showed us how we could love a place and
want to change it at the same time." Willie was eulogized from the
floor of the U.S. House of Representatives and in the Senate.

Many recalled his sweetness, his big-heartedness, his encouragement of fledgling writers, his inspiring of all people to be creative, his
attachment to children, animals, and the elderly, his pervasive humor
and his boylike fondness for pranks. Comparisons to Mark Twain,
to Huck Finn and Tom Sawyer, abounded. "He could get someone
else to paint his fence in a heartbeat," Malcolm White says, "and you
thought it was the most fun you'd had in your life." Willie was also
remembered for his easy way of making a friend feel special and for
his genius of seeing inside another's heart to discern what mattered.
And he was remembered for his fierce intellect and his master storytelling, for his complicated love of the South and for "turn[ing] his
childhood in Yazoo City, Miss., into a place almost as complex and
resonant as William Faulkner's Yoknapatawpha County." Many said,
simply, that they would miss him, this man known to everyone as
"Willie."

He hadn't finished his novels *The Chimes at Midnight* or *Taps*. He hadn't become the novelist he'd aspired to be, but he had left an impressive legacy in nonfiction writing. He had done this while at the University of Texas, where he fought for editorial freedom for his student newspaper, and he did this during his celebrated editorship of *Harper's*, where he gave his writers rein to experiment with nontraditional language and journalistic forms. In his articles and books, he wove material from his own life together with his deep understanding of history to reflect on issues, such as racism, that were important for the South and the nation. As an unavowed intellectual, he challenged the South and pushed it forward, but as a self-professed good old boy, he did so with affection and compassion for his fellow southerners.

Often his writing was rooted in the predilections and legends of his beloved hometown, and he wrote lyrically and nostalgically, with generosity and a gently humorous spirit, about dogs and witches, country boys, and giant warriors. He may not have become the novelist he wanted to be, but much like the Old Scotchman in his baseball play-by-play, Willie sometimes "made pristine facts more actual than reality," embellishing his stories, enhancing their truths, in the process making art and making that small town eternally his. "A place belongs forever to whoever claims it hardest," Joan Didion once wrote, "remembers it most obsessively, wrenches it from itself, shapes it, renders it, loves it so radically that he remakes it in his image." That was Willie and his Yazoo: claiming it, remembering it, wrenching it, shaping it, rendering it, and ultimately remaking it to fit the image in his prodigious memory.

Over the next several years, publishers would bring out the last books that Willie had finished before his death. In November of 1999, Random House published *My Cat Spit McGee*. The memoir was widely reviewed, receiving generally good notices, with Jonathan Yardley in the *Washington Post* judging it "funny and endearing." The following fall, the University Press issued *My Mississippi*, Willie's millennial appraisal of his home state, with ninety-five color photographs by David Rae Morris.

New editions of Willie's books continued to appear, along with tributes and compilations of his essays and interviews. For what would have been his sixty-fifth birthday, the University Press of

Mississippi reissued *North Toward Home* in hardcover; later, Vintage Books would publish it in paperback. *Remembering Willie*, a collection of eulogies and accolades by his friends, from writers to politicians, came out from the University Press, as did *Conversations with Willie Morris*, consisting of interviews that spanned over thirty years. The press also published a selection of Willie's essays, *Shifting Interludes*, and for the seventy-fifth anniversary of his birth, a gift edition of *My Two Oxfords*.

But not only Willie's books kept him before the public: the movie of *My Dog Skip* premiered the winter following his death. *Skip* grossed over $35 million and, due to its relatively small budget, proved one of that year's most profitable releases; both the Broadcast Film Critics Association and the Christophers named it Best Family Film. Symposia were also given in Willie's honor. In 2000, the University of Mississippi dedicated its annual Oxford Conference for the Book to him. In subsequent years, Yazoo City, in the brick schoolhouse that he had once attended, hosted "Remembering Willie," with talks and readings by his fellow writers and friends. Upstairs in that same building, in the Sam B. Olden Yazoo Historical Society Museum, an exhibit was later mounted with mementoes from Willie's life, including Skip's marble tombstone.

Just a few days after his death, Yazoo City officials had made a public resolution in appreciation of Willie, proclaiming that he had "distinguished himself and Yazoo City through his unique ability to capture and convey the essence of the Southern spirit." Although some had been upset initially by Willie's portrayal of Yazoo City in *North Toward Home*, for many years he had been on excellent terms with his hometown. He once said, in his inimitable way, and with a flash of humor, "When you write a book in which you draw on a place that is really identifiable—and this is not just Southern, this is quite American—they hate your guts for about twenty years, and then they name a street after you." In 2015, Yazoo City began construction of the Willie Morris Parkway.

Other institutions have honored Willie. At the University of Texas, more than fifty of his brothers at Delta Tau Delta fraternity contributed to furnishing a study room in his name, including copies of his books, his portrait, and a plaque recognizing "his courage to speak out for reform and to protest injustice." Fraternity brother Dave Williams, along with his wife Reba White Williams, founded the annual Willie Morris Award for Southern Fiction, which as of 2016 is in its ninth year. In 2006, in Jackson, the modern, light-filled Willie Morris Library was opened on a wooded lot next to an oxbow lake, not far from the house that he had shared with JoAnne. The dedication took place on what would have been Willie's seventy-second birthday. "Happy Birthday" was played on a trombone, and the crowd joined in. "Willie would have been pleased," wrote his friend, journalist Bill Minor, "a library in the woods named for him . . . To use one of his favorite words: ineffable."

◆ ◆ ◆

A month after Willie's death, JoAnne wrote to an old friend of his in Austin. "The numbness has worn off now, and I'm dealing with the reality that Willie is really gone." She turned her attention to his last request to "get *Taps* together." He had left a manuscript with handwritten notes in the margins, enumerating the changes that he one day wanted to make. In an interview in *Publishers Weekly*, JoAnne described her work on *Taps* as editing, or in the words of Eudora Welty, "putting the moon in the right part of the sky." JoAnne would eventually write in the novel's acknowledgments, "Although I had some hesitation about becoming immersed in the work so soon after his death, this experience was ultimately a uniquely fulfilling one—a sweet and lovely conversation with Willie. As always, I learned much from him about words and life, and even more about his tender, sorrowful, loving, full heart."

Willie's agent, Theron Raines, placed *Taps* with Houghton Mifflin, the Boston firm that had been Willie's first publisher all those years ago. At the novel's heart is young Swayze Barksdale, of fictional Fisk's Landing, Mississippi, who plays "Taps" at the military funerals of Korean War soldiers. In his small town poised on the edge of change, he comes to learn much about the loss of a first love and the ache of passing from adolescence to adulthood. Houghton Mifflin brought the novel out in the spring of 2001, planning an ambitious printing of fifty thousand copies; the publisher sent JoAnne on a six-city tour, where she was joined by Willie's friends David Halberstam and William Styron. The novel received much attention and many reviews, the majority positive, although some key newspapers, such as the *New York Times*, were mixed in their assessments.

With JoAnne's help, Willie had at last realized *Taps*, his "baby," the novel that he believed contained all he knew. It had been his lifetime in the making. In the book's last paragraph, set in the old cemetery, Willie gives his protagonist Swayze the final word on his life, his art, and his town:

> I have a vivid recurring dream of an echo. I am standing alone under the magnolia tree as the mourners disperse below. The old veterans have stacked their rifles. Potter and Woodrow are folding the chairs. The gravediggers have reappeared from their hidden places. Soon four figures gradually approach me from the lower sweep of the hill. At first they are dim and indistinct. Through a diaphanous mist I try to make them out. They come closer, and then they find me and stand lovingly before me: Georgia and Luke and Amanda and Dusty! I am with them again, and the accumulated past rises before me, and, beyond, the town itself, in all its sad and wonderful seasons, and the consuming earth where we briefly lived. And now I see that the earth—this restless, powerful land—is gentle too in its eternal promise of a place where all our troubled kind can rest when day is done.

Acknowledgments

———❦———

I FIRST WOULD LIKE TO THANK JOHN LANGSTON, ART DIRECTOR extraordinaire at the University Press of Mississippi, for encouraging me to write this book. John has been a creative inspiration since we were coeditors of our high school newspaper, the *Yazooan*, and he remains my dear longtime friend.

My profound thanks to JoAnne Prichard Morris and David Rae Morris, for the hours of interviews and the many follow-up emails and telephone calls, for providing letters, photos, and memorabilia, and for reading and commenting on the manuscript. Both have been generous with their time and enthusiastic about the biography from the beginning.

I owe a debt of gratitude to Celia Morris, who shared her insights with me in Austin and who later provided more specifics in emails and who read portions of the manuscript.

This book has been a collaboration with some of the many friends that Willie made and kept throughout his life, and beyond. They have been unstinting with their recollections in interviews and emails, and I would like to thank them especially: Wayne Agnew, Shaye Areheart, Bob and Amanda Cary Bailey, Jimmie Ball, Benjamin "B" Barrier, Jean Baskin, Ron Borne, Jill Conner Browne, Dan Burck, Hunter Cole, Fletcher and Carol Cox, Jim Dees, Ronnie Dugger, Nadine Eckhardt, John Evans, Ray Farabee, William Ferris, Anne Glover, Robert Gottlieb, Margaret Pepper Grantham, Thomas and Carol Hatfield, Cary Hill, Karen Hinton, Barbera Hollowell Liddon, Richard Howorth, Henry Jacoby, Jamie Jones, Kaylie Jones, Harold and Hannah Kelly, Harriet DeCell Kuykendall, Jack Little, Robert

Loomis, William H. Morris Jr., Gerald Moses, Will Norton, Sam B. Olden, Sam Perry, Jon Abner Reeves, Sid Salter, David Sansing, Ron Shapiro, Malcolm White, Curtis Wilkie, Dave Williams, Marsha Dunn Williams, Ruth Williams, Willard "Bill" Wyman, Steve Yarbrough, and Edwin M. Yoder Jr.

In addition, my thanks go to André Baltimore, Jack Bales, Bobby Barton, Helene Berinsky, Roger Brudno, Nettie Clark Byrd, Cecil Cartwright, Tom Davis, Celia Dugger, Howard and Cynthia Epstein, Samuel Hall, Andy Hughes, Susannah Jacob, Martha Kaplan, Kate McCorkle, Chuck McIntosh, Norman Mott Jr., Deirdre Mullane, Danny Nicholas, Jason Patterson, Alan Pogue, Helen Rattray, D. B. "Doc" Rushing, Miriam Schneir, Lou Schwartz, Larry Wells, Rick Wendling, and Bill Woodell for assistance with my research and for encouragement while I was writing the book.

I am grateful for permission to examine the nearly twenty thousand letters in the Willie Morris Collection in Archives and Special Collections at the J. D. Williams Library at the University of Mississippi. I want to thank Jennifer Ford, Head of Special Collections and Associate Professor, and her amiable, helpful staff, including Jessica Leming, Visual Collections Librarian. I would also like to thank, in Yazoo City, John E. Ellzey at B. S. Ricks Memorial Library; at the University of Texas, the staffs of the Dolph Briscoe Center for American History, the Perry-Castañeda Library, and the Collections Deposit Library; at the University of North Carolina, the staff of the Louis Round Wilson Special Collections Library; in Jackson, the employees of the Willie Morris Library and the Mississippi Department of Archives and History, and the *Clarion-Ledger*.

Thank you very much to my editor at the University Press of Mississippi, Leila Salisbury, and the entire staff of the press. They are a dedicated and talented group who have contributed much to the arts and letters of this state. Thanks also to my friend Mark McCauslin for proofreading. I am greatly indebted to Dave and Reba White Williams for their financial assistance with the production of this book.

Finally, I wish to thank my family—my aunt Willie Belle Hood, who never failed to ask me about my progress, and my sisters Debbie and Lisa Nicholas; Lisa provided me with wise editorial counsel, for which I am indebted. But I am grateful most of all to my husband, the writer and editor Gerard Helferich, who helped with research and editing while supplying moral propping up as I tried to capture the complexities of Willie's personality between book covers. Thank you for our writing life. Thank you for our life together.

Chronology of Willie Morris's Life

1934   William Weaks Morris born to Henry Rae Morris and Marion Harper Weaks Morris on Thanksgiving Day, November 29, in Jackson, Mississippi.

1935   The Morris family moves to Yazoo City.

1948–52   Willie attends Yazoo City High School, where he edits the *Flashlight*, the school newspaper.

1952–56   Attends the University of Texas in Austin. In March 1955 wins the Clarence E. Gilmore Award for his article in the *Daily Texan* "Here's What to Do When a Tornado Hits." Assumes editorship of the *Daily Texan* in June 1955. Graduates from the university with high honors and is elected to Phi Beta Kappa.

1956–60   Attends Oxford University as a Rhodes Scholar.

1958   Marries Celia Ann Buchan on August 30 in Houston, Texas. Father, Henry Rae Morris, dies on September 2 in Yazoo City.

1959   Son, David Rae Morris, born on November 1 in Oxford, England.

1960–62   Editor on the *Texas Observer* in Austin, Texas. Becomes editor-in-chief in early 1961.

1963   Joins the staff of *Harper's* magazine in New York City as associate editor.

1965   Becomes executive editor of *Harper's*. Edits special supplement "The South Today."

1967–71   Editor-in-chief of *Harper's* magazine. Publishes groundbreaking articles by William Styron, Norman Mailer, Gay Talese, David Halberstam, Seymour Hersh, and others.

1967   Publishes his memoir *North Toward Home*, which wins the Houghton Mifflin Literary Fellowship Award and the

Texas Institute of Letters Carr P. Collins Award for Best Nonfiction Book.

1969   Divorce from Celia Morris becomes final.

1971   Resigns from *Harper's* magazine and relocates to Bridge-hampton, New York, to devote himself to writing fulltime. Publishes *Good Old Boy*, which wins the Texas Institute of Letters' Steck-Vaughn Award for Best Children's Book.

1974   Grandmother Marion "Mamie" Harper Weaks dies on February 15 in Yazoo City.

1977   Mother, Marion Harper Weaks Morris, dies on April 15 in Yazoo City.

1980–91 Writer-in-residence at the University of Mississippi.

1983   Publishes *The Courting of Marcus Dupree*, which receives a Christopher Award.

1989   Publishes *Homecomings*, which receives the Authors Award for nonfiction from the Mississippi Library Association.

1990   Marries JoAnne Prichard on September 14 in Jackson.

1993   Publishes *New York Days*, which wins the nonfiction award from the Mississippi Institute of Arts and Letters.

1994   Receives the Governor's Arts Award from the Mississippi Arts Commission.

1995   Publishes *My Dog Skip*.

1996   Wins the Richard Wright Medal for Literary Excellence from the Natchez (MS) Literary and Cinema Celebration.

1998   Publishes *The Ghosts of Medgar Evers*. Filming of the movie *My Dog Skip* begins.

1999   Dies of heart failure on August 2 in Jackson, at age sixty-four. Buried in Glenwood Cemetery in Yazoo City.

2000   The movie of *My Dog Skip* premieres and wins Best Family Film from the Broadcast Film Critics Association and the Christophers.

2001   Novel *Taps* is published posthumously.

Books by Willie Morris

1965 *The South Today: One Hundred Years After Appomattox* (edited and with a foreword by Willie Morris)
1967 *North Toward Home*
1971 *Yazoo: Integration in a Deep-Southern Town*
1971 *Good Old Boy: A Delta Boyhood*
1973 *The Last of the Southern Girls*
1975 *A Southern Album: Recollections of Some People and Places and Times Gone By* (edited by Irwin Glusker and narrative by Willie Morris)
1978 *James Jones: A Friendship*
1981 *Terrains of the Heart and Other Essays on Home*
1983 *The Courting of Marcus Dupree*
1983 *Always Stand In Against the Curve*
1989 *Good Old Boy and the Witch of Yazoo*
1989 *Homecomings*
1990 *Faulkner's Mississippi*
1992 *My Two Oxfords*
1992 *After All, It's Only a Game*
1993 *New York Days*
1995 *My Dog Skip*
1995 *A Prayer for the Opening of the Little League Season*
1998 *The Ghosts of Medgar Evers: A Tale of Race, Murder, Mississippi, and Hollywood*

POSTHUMOUS PUBLICATIONS

1999 *My Cat Spit McGee*
2000 *My Mississippi*
2001 *Taps*
2002 *Shifting Interludes*

Sources

9   Morris family's early years in Yazoo City: interview with Sam B. Olden; email from Nettie Clark Byrd.

9   Willie's scarlet fever episode: *North Toward Home*, p. 8; interview with JoAnne Prichard Morris.

9   "The child Dr. Miller saved": *North Toward Home*, p. 9.

9   Date of Morris family's move and mortgage: Yazoo County Property Records.

10   Description of Morris house: Johnson; interviews with JoAnne Prichard Morris, Margaret Pepper Grantham, Amanda Cary Bailey.

10   "Like Mr. Mozart": *North Toward Home*, p. 18.

10   Willie's piano lessons, including quotations: Morris 2002, p. 36.

10   Harper family history, including quotations: *North Toward Home*, pp. 10–14; O'Beirne. There is doubt about whether Sherman's army actually destroyed Harper's printing presses.

11   Willie's visits to his Jackson relatives, including quotations: *North Toward Home*, pp. 57–65; interview with JoAnne Prichard Morris. In *North Toward Home*, Willie misstates Percy and Sue's birthdates; Percy's correct date appears on findagrave.com, and Sue's appears in O'Beirne.

11   Willie and his father's baseball outings: Morris 2002, p. 35 (including quotation); Bales 2006, p. 17.

12   Willie's hunting and fishing: *North Toward Home*, pp. 72–76.

12   "Ours was a nonverbal relation": Morris 2002, p. 36.

12   "My Negro nurse": *North Toward Home*, pp. 39–40.

12   Willie's preschool years: interviews with and emails from Margaret Pepper Grantham; Grantham (film, see bibliography); interview with Sam B. Olden.

13   St. Clara's Academy history: DeCell, p. 367.

13   Buba Barrier: Willie spells his friend's name "Bubba" in *North Toward Home*, but Barrier has always spelled it "Buba."

TWO: SCHOOL DAYS IN YAZOO: "A PLEASANT, DRIFTLESS LIFE"

14   "A pleasant, driftless life": *North Toward Home*, p. 127.

14   Willie's early schooling: *North Toward Home*, pp. 18–19, 21–24, 26–27, 29–30, including all quotations not otherwise attributed; interviews and emails from Margaret Pepper Grantham, Amanda Cary Bailey, JoAnne Prichard Morris.

14   Characterization of Morris family life: interviews with JoAnne Prichard Morris and Jimmie Ball.

15   "She stayed on him": interview with Jimmie Ball.

15   "Oh, I remember": email from Margaret Pepper Grantham.

15–17 Willie's after-school activities and pranks: *North Toward Home*, pp. 29–31, 34–36, 62–63, including all quotations not otherwise cited; interviews and emails from Margaret Pepper Grantham, Jimmie Ball, JoAnne Prichard Morris, Amanda Cary Bailey.

18   "I stood in front of the open coffin": *North Toward Home*, p. 66.

18   "As a kind of consolation prize": *North Toward Home*, p. 67.

18   "I was an only child" and "for the lively way he walked": Morris 1995, p. 4.

18   "In case of accident," "Skip is smart," and "Skip is still smart": unpublished childhood diary.

18   Skip's squirrel chasing: interview with Jimmie Ball.

18   "I cut the lace on a football": *North Toward Home*, p. 68.

18   "Look at that dog playin' football!": *North Toward Home*, p. 69.

18   "Anywhere that white adults were not likely to spot us": *North Toward Home*, p. 31.

19   "Hey, look at me" and description of Skip "driving": interview with Margaret Pepper Grantham.

19   Baseball in Yazoo City: *North Toward Home*, pp. 101–23; interview with Gerald Moses.

19   "Like Mark Twain and his comrades": *North Toward Home*, pp. 101–2.

19   "Shiny blue jackets": *North Toward Home*, p. 121.

20   "They finally quit the program": interview with Jimmie Ball.

20   "Even among the adults": *North Toward Home*, p. 104.

20   "A weapon of unimaginable dimensions" and "instead of being disappointed": *North Toward Home*, p. 112.

21   Glenwood Cemetery, including Willie's bet with Jon Abner Reeves: *North Toward Home*, pp. 31–34; interviews with Margaret Pepper Grantham, Jon Abner Reeves, and Jimmie Ball. Willie spells his victim's name "John," but it is actually "Jon." Also, John Hancock had no grandchildren.

21–22 Willie's early attitude toward race relations, including quotations: *North Toward Home*, pp. 77–78, 86; interview with JoAnne Prichard Morris.

22   Mamie Harper Weaks's moderate attitude on race: Bales 2000, p. 158.

22–23 Willie's high school matriculation and academics, including all quotations unless otherwise noted: *North Toward Home*, pp. 124, 127, 135–36; interviews with and emails from Margaret Pepper Grantham.

23   "We were above average": interview with Margaret Pepper Grantham.

23–24 Willie's extracurricular activities and "left fielder Willie Morris": *Mingo Chito*, 1952.

24   "A good student of the game": interview with Harold Kelly.

24   Willie's tenure on the *Flashlight*: *Flashlight*, 1949–52; *North Toward Home*, pp. 130–31, 141; *Mingo Chito*, 1951 and 1952; "'Flashlight' Cops National Awards in Press Contests," *Flashlight*, May 29, 1952.

25   Willie's early journalism and radio experience: *North Toward Home*, pp. 103, 131–32; Bales 2000, p. 163.

25–26 Willie's trumpet playing, including "played for more funerals": *North Toward Home*, pp. 93–95.

26   "An echo, I would learn"; Morris 2001, p. 36.

26   "He wanted to write the truth" and "This made me think": emails from Margaret Pepper Grantham.

26–27 Willie's social life: interviews with and emails from Margaret Pepper Grantham; *North Toward Home*, pp. 127–28, 138–39.

27 Willie and friends' high school awards and honors: *Mingo Chito*, 1952; Class of 1952 Yazoo City High School graduation program; despite what Willie wrote in *North Toward Home*, there is no mention of an official class valedictorian.

27 Willie's graduation and his and his friends' college plans: *North Toward Home*, pp. 140–45; "Seniors Tell Their Future; Majority Will Attend School," "Party-Poopers Play Paltry Parts; Pickled 'til June"; "55 Senior Graduates Receive Sheepskins," all from the *Flashlight*, May 29, 1952.

27–28 "The best and certainly the biggest state university," "dug right out of stone," and "something different was stirring": *North Toward Home*, p. 143.

28 "The crowd had departed": *Flashlight*, May 29, 1952.

THREE: "READY TO LICK THIS OLD WORLD": THE UNIVERSITY OF TEXAS

29 "Ready to lick this old world": *Daily Texan*, September 17, 1952.

29 "It took me years to understand": *North Toward Home*, p. 165.

29 "One cold dark morning": *North Toward Home*, p. 144.

29 Willie's likely bus route: emails from Dr. D. B. "Doc" Rushing, webmaster of "Blue-hounds and Redhounds, the History of Greyhound and Trailways" (bluehounds andredhounds.info).

30 Number of UT students in the early 1950s: University of Texas website (utexas .edu).

30 Willie's arrival in Austin: *North Toward Home*, p. 151 (including "emerged from that bus"); interviews with Wayne Agnew (including "like a child" and "I'm hungry") and Thomas Hatfield.

30 Willie's classes: University of Texas transcript.

30 "I myself shared that compulsion": *North Toward Home*, p. 153.

31 Willie's activities freshman year: interview with Thomas Hatfield and Dave Williams; *Cactus*, 1953; *North Toward Home*, p. 153; *Daily Texan*, April 27, 1955; *Daily Texan*, November 6, 1955. Willie may also have played on the freshman baseball team, but his participation is difficult to document.

31 Willie's commitment to print journalism: letter to Robert Loomis, July 12, 1999; courtesy JoAnne Prichard Morris.

31 History of the *Daily Texan*: Copp, pp. 12, 20, 35–36, 62–64.

31 "Its physical set-up was impressive": *North Toward Home*, p. 162.

32 Letter of reference from Omie Parker: Bales 2006, p. 27.

32 Willie's first article: *Daily Texan*, September 17, 1952.

32–33 Willie's first "Neighboring News" column: *Daily Texan*, September 18, 1952.

33 "Here I began to read" and "I gradually began to see": *North Toward Home*, pp. 162–63.

33   Willie's three new *Daily Texan* tasks: *Cactus*, 1953; *Daily Texan*, April 1, 1953; *Daily Texan*, April 8, 1953.

33–34   Willie's experiences in Brackenridge Hall and the Delta Tau Delta fraternity house: interview with Thomas Hatfield; *North Toward Home*, pp. 158–60 (including quotations).

34   Frank Lyell background: University of Texas website.

34   "My dog Skip and I wandered" and "the power not merely of language": *North Toward Home*, pp. 165–66.

34–35   "More books than I had ever seen," "it is a rare experience," "be a writer," "to read every important book," and "but once this fire is lit": *North Toward Home*, p. 164.

35   "Brought all of his books": interview with Jack Little.

35   "Hankman, why don't you read this?": interview with Henry Jacoby.

35   "The acceptance of ideas": *North Toward Home*, p. 150.

36   "The Flow of Life and Time": *Daily Texan*, February 11, 1954.

36   "Some impalpable force": *Daily Texan*, May 14, 1954.

36   Willie's membership in Goodfellows and Silver Spurs: *Cactus*, 1954.

37   "Sportswriters were often at the heart": Copp, p. 67.

37   Bevo's journey to Notre Dame, including quotations: *Daily Texan*, September 29, 1954; *Daily Texan*, September 21, 1954; *Daily Texan*, September 24, 1954; interview with Dan Burck, who accompanied Willie on the trip. Burck went on to become a successful businessman and chancellor of the University of Texas. Dean Smith had won a gold medal in track in the 1952 Olympics and later became a Hollywood stuntman.

37   "Greet adulthood": *Daily Texan*, October 20, 1954.

38   "Only a patient and comradely approach": *Daily Texan*, December 5, 1954.

38   "Infectious gaiety": Celia Morris, p. 68.

38   Celia Morris's attraction to Willie: interview with Celia Morris.

38   Willie's campaign for editor: *North Toward Home*, pp. 175–76; interview with Dave Williams. "Landslide": *Daily Texan*, April 27, 1955. The tally was 3,357 to 1,914.

38   "It was a viciously hot Texas afternoon": *North Toward Home*, p. 180.

39   "That it will always fight for progress and reform": Morris 1993, p. 8.

39   "A NEW YEAR begins today" and subsequent quotations: Morris, "A New Year for the *Texan*—We'll Play Hard and Clean," *Daily Texan*, June 7, 1955.

40   Celia Morris's travels in Europe: interview with Celia Morris.

40   "Would have lifelong repercussions": Celia Morris, p. 71.

40   Willie's course load and summer activities: Transcript, University of Texas; *North Toward Home*, pp. 180–81.

40   "Ramshackle Plymouth" and "had the most overwhelming sense": *North Toward Home*, p. 176.

40   Petition and aftermath, including quotations: "'Non-Discriminatory Basis' NAACP Asks School Board," *Yazoo City Herald*, August 18, 1955; "Public Invited to Meeting

of Citizens Council Friday," *Yazoo City Herald*, August 25, 1955; "Only 6 Names Left on List; Lions to Hear 'Tut' Patterson," *Yazoo City Herald*, September 1, 1955.

40   "I knew in that instant": *North Toward Home*, p. 180.

41   Willie's grueling schedule: interviews with Carol Hatfield and Henry Jacoby.

41   "The real things": *Daily Texan*, November 11, 1955.

41   "We drank a quart of California wine": *North Toward Home*, p. 173; Celia's inscription was from a poem by Robert Browning. In that book Willie writes that this took place on his twentieth birthday, but in *Shifting Interludes* he says it was on his twenty-first. I believe this later account is correct.

41   "Yet there were to be" and "unusual things": *North Toward Home*, pp. 183–84.

42   "We feel *The Daily Texan*" and "We just want to hold [Willie]": *Daily Texan*, February 9, 1956.

42   "A strong believer" and "the Yankees threw": "The Round-Up," *Daily Texan*, June 7, 1955.

42   "Influence the outcome": *Daily Texan*, February 8, 1956.

42   Willie's editorials during *Daily Texan* controversy: February 28, 1956; February 9, 1956; February 8, 1956.

42–43 For Willie's account of the dispute with the Regents, see his essay "Mississippi Rebel on a Texas Campus" in the *Nation*, March 24, 1956, reprinted in Morris 2002. For more on J. Frank Dobie's defense of the *Daily Texan*, see "Dobie Blasts Regents," *Daily Texan*, February 9, 1956. For an example of Ronnie Dugger's editorials in favor of the *Daily Texan*, see "Death of the Texan," reprinted in the *Daily Texan*, April 17, 1956.

43   "As much concerned with free intellectual enterprise": As quoted in *North Toward Home*, p. 190.

43   "The issue is not how the *Texan* feels": "Prerogative of Dissent Defended by Texan," *Daily Texan*, February 9, 1956.

43   "The necessity of the free marketplace" and "teach those of us": *North Toward Home*, pp. 186, 150–51.

44   "Charmin' Celia Cradles Campus Crown": *Daily Texan*, April 8, 1956.

44   "Five thousand people sang": *North Toward Home*, pp. 172–73.

44   "Vivacious personality": Couch.

FOUR: "LEAPING AND LINGERING": FROM OXFORD TO THE *OBSERVER*

45   "Leaping and lingering": interview with Willard "Bill" Wyman.

45   "It had been the freest time of my life": Morris 2009, p. 19.

45   "A rather bewildered-looking fellow": interview with Edwin M. Yoder Jr.

45   "Brothers really": Yoder, p. 204.

45   Willie's arrival in England: Yoder, pp. 66–67.

46   "Multifarious vehicles and grinding motors": Morris 2002, p. 131.

46   "Antiquarian booksellers and numismatists": Morris 1993, p. 238.

46   "Entering the gateways": Morris 2002, p. 132.

47   "Had been new in 1379": Morris 1993, p. 48.

47   "In a little room": Bales 2000, p. 32.

47   "Older than the discovery" and "a long way, too long": *North Toward Home*, pp. 195–96.

47   Willie and Ed Yoder's culinary fantasies: Yoder, p. 78.

47   "The sacrosanct privacy of the place": Morris 2009, p. 3.

47   "Oh to be in April": *North Toward Home*, p. 195. The original Robert Browning poem reads, "Oh, to be in England/Now that April's there."

47   "Obscure and low-ceiled tavern": Hardy, p. 87. The novel was first published as a serial in *Harper's New Monthly Magazine* from December 1894 to November 1895.

48   "I wandered alone": Morris 1995, pp. 121–22. Skip's tombstone can be seen in the Sam B. Olden Yazoo Historical Society Museum in Yazoo City.

48   "Why don't you all get another fox terrier?": undated letter, Willie Morris Collection, Archives and Special Collections, University of Mississippi Libraries. His parents did not get another fox terrier.

48   "Slowly, the spell of Oxford grew": Morris 1993, p. 41.

48   "So enamoured of that haunting, beautiful place": *North Toward Home*, p. 195.

48   "One of the English students": Morris 2009, p. 4.

48–49 "I had stayed up straight" and "quiet and detached": *North Toward Home*, p. 195.

49   Willie's extracurricular activities and social life at Oxford: Morris 1993, pp. 44–45; Bales 2006, p. 163; Morris 2002, p. 143, Morris 1981, p. 87.

49   "Carried his clothes and books": Yoder, p. 193.

49   "Almost as long as a hearse": WM to his parents, undated, Willie Morris Collection. Willie wrote an essay about this trip called "The John Foster Dulles"; see Morris 2002, p. 197.

49–50 Willie's father's illness and death: *Yazoo City Herald*, September 4, 1958.

49   Willie and Celia's engagement: Celia Morris, p. 84; email from Celia Morris.

50   Willie and Celia's wedding: *Yazoo City Herald*, August 21, 1958.

50   Willie and Celia's life in Oxford: Celia Morris, pp. 90–94.

50   "His face to the wall": Celia Morris, p. 87.

50   Celia's gratitude to Willie and feelings of distance: Celia Morris, p. 93.

50   Willie's studies at Oxford: Bales 2000, p. 66. In 1966, Willie was awarded a master of arts degree by Oxford; this is a degree conferred seven years after graduation without any further examinations, on the payment of certain fees.

50–51 "In a big dusty house," "a top-floor flat," "a big Texas man," "82 cents," "the English operator phoned back," and "waterlogged with the past": *North Toward Home*, pp. 196–97.

51   Willie was in the delivery room, and Celia had a cold: email from David Rae Morris.

51   The novel that Willie was writing then was never published; Willie claimed to have burned the manuscript (Bales 2000, p. 62).

51 "Easily the most celebrated": Yoder, p. 205.

51–52 "It had been the freest time": Morris 2009, p. 19.

52 Willie and Celia's journey to Austin and house rental: *North Toward Home*, p. 198; Celia Morris, p. 106.

52 "Independent and liberal alternative": email from Ronnie Dugger.

52 "Hardcore right-wing newspapers": interview with Ronnie Dugger.

52 "We will serve no group": *Texas Observer* website, texasobserver.org.

52 "Underlined it with a ball-point pen": *North Toward Home*, p. 202.

52 "Fighting liberal editor" and "That's what attracted me": interview with Ronnie Dugger.

52–53 "Not only one of the great reporters": *North Toward Home*, p. 200.

53 Ronnie taught Willie how to be a reporter: interview with JoAnne Prichard Morris.

53 Willie's coverage of 1960 election: *North Toward Home*, pp. 233–42.

53 "Soon, Willie will become editor": *Texas Observer*, December 16, 1960.

53 "Absolute editorial control": interview with Ronnie Dugger.

53 "Was probably the toughest": Bales 2000, p. 63.

53 "Always there were the stories to cover": *North Toward Home*, p. 247.

54 "New gang": Celia Morris, p. 107.

54–55 Celia's depiction of her marriage, life in Austin, and career: Celia Morris, pp. 115–22.

55 "Run out of gas": *North Toward Home*, p. 310.

55 Willie's job offer at *Harper's*, "Quite frankly I'm looking around for a successor" and "read, reflect": Morris 1993, pp. 15–18. Willie's quotation is from memory. He writes two different versions of the events surrounding the letter from John Fischer. In *North Toward Home* he says he took the Greyhound to New York and had several interviews, including one with Fischer at *Harper's*. In *New York Days*, he says he received the letter from Fischer while still living in Austin. I believe the latter version, which Willie corroborated in an interview with Jack Bales in *Conversations with Willie Morris*, is correct.

55 56 Willie's time in Palo Alto: Morris 1993, pp. 19–20; Bales 2000, pp. 170–71.

56 "I would say Willie was trying to find himself": interview with Willard "Bill" Wyman.

56 "All the important junctures": *North Toward Home*, p. 313.

FIVE: THE *HARPER'S* YEARS: REACHING THE "ORGANIZATIONAL SUMMIT"

57 "Organizational summit": Morris 1993, p. 364.

57 "There were eight million telephone numbers": Morris 1993, p. 4.

57 Willie's likely bus route: emails from Dr. D. B. "Doc" Rushing.

57 "Indulge in glamorous fantasies," "soft spring evening," and "we had always come": *North Toward Home*, pp. 315, 317, 318.

58   "Crossroads": Samuel S. Vaughn, editor-in-chief of Doubleday, as quoted in McDowell.

58   "Pluperfect hick": *North Toward Home*, p. 327.

58   Willie's salary at *Harper's*: *North Toward Home*, p. 332.

58   Average family income in New York City: U.S. Department of Labor, Bureau of Labor Statistics (bls.gov).

58–59 Willie and Celia's apartment hunting: *North Toward Home*, pp. 320–21, 333.

59   Description of apartment: email from David Rae Morris.

59   "Approximately the dimensions": Morris 1993, p. 22.

59   Willie's early responsibilities at *Harper's*: Morris 1993, pp. 32–36.

59   Celia's apartment hunting: Celia Morris, p. 139.

59   "Grungy and ravaged": Morris 1993, p. 62.

59   For Willie, the 1960s began in 1962: Morris 1993, pp. 16–17.

60   "The center was not holding": Joan Didion, *Slouching Towards Bethlehem*, as quoted in Morris 1993, p. 70. Didion's phrase is an allusion to the William Butler Yeats poem "The Second Coming"; her book title is from the same source.

60   "First full-fledged literary cocktail party": *North Toward Home*, p. 355.

61   "Frosty politeness": *North Toward Home*, p. 359.

61   "Exiles" and "alienated from home": *North Toward Home*, pp. 319–20.

61   "*Southernness*": *North Toward Home*, p. 384.

61   "Where else in the East but in Harlem": *North Toward Home*, p. 387.

61   "Somewhat remote and docile," "grindingly arid," "red hot center," and "Squaresville": Morris 1993, pp. 37, 30, 23, and 23, respectively.

61   Fischer began training Willie: Morris 1993, p. 29.

61   "Harsh," "cliquish," and "mean as hell": *North Toward Home*, p. 400.

62   "Illuminate for non-Southerners the interaction of North and South": *Harper's*, April 1965, p. 126.

63   Willie and Celia's life together, including quotations: Celia Morris, pp. 132–55.

63–64 "America is changing": Text of speech courtesy JoAnne Prichard Morris.

64   "The primary responsibility for editorial direction": *Harper's*, July 1967.

64   Cowles's purchase of *Harper's*, including "interested in making profits": Kihss.

64   Willie and Cowles's plan for *Harper's*: Morris 1993, pp. 8–10 (including quotations), 81; Shnayerson.

64   Willie believed he was promised five years: King 2006, p. 145.

65   "Lively and relevant if sometimes irreverent," "a stronger appeal for younger readers," and "truly *national* magazine": Morris 1993, p. 9.

65   "Pursued relentlessly": Morris 1993, p. 81.

65   "Write about that for me": King 1987, p. 63.

65   "Willie wanted you to write": Corry, p. 29.

66   "When the word got out": Morris 1993, p. 75.

66   "An autobiography in mid-passage": publisher's press release, March 1967; courtesy B. S. Ricks Memorial Library.

67 "No one at age thirty-two": as quoted by Rebecca Bain, in Bales 2000, p. 183.

67 "On the whole Morris gives us": Madison Jones.

67 "The finest evocation": *Sunday Times* (London), as quoted on the cover of the Vintage Books edition, 2000.

67 "The biggest event": Morris 1993, p. 79.

67 "Through the medium of ridicule and exaggerations": Collins.

67 "See my book for what it is": *Yazoo City Herald*, October 19, 1967.

67–68 "There were eight million telephone numbers" and "I sat next to DiMaggio": Morris 1993, p. 4.

68 "After-work gossip and plotting" and "interminable cocktails": Morris 1993, p. 11.

68 "I drank too much, ate too much, talked too much": Morris 1993, pp. 152–53.

68 Willie and Cowles's decision to pay Styron more: Morris 1993, pp. 125–26.

68 "A literary genius": Morris 1993, p. 211.

68 "The Steps of the Pentagon" publication: Morris 1993, pp. 214–22.

69 "'The Steps of the Pentagon' was in every aspect": Morris 1993, p. 222.

70 "Under the editorship of Willie Morris": Decter, p. 61.

70 "Aroused, interested, and engaged": Willie Morris Collection, WM to William Blair, 2/17/71.

70 "More than any other journalist": interview with and email from Ronnie Dugger.

70 "The Prisoner of Sex" sold more newsstand copies: Morris 1993, p. 355.

71 "We are anxious to do all," "make every continuing effort," "very false and misleading economy," "four alternatives," "I will never, under any circumstances," and "I will do everything I can": Willie Morris Collection, WM to William Blair, 2/17/71.

71–72 Willie's meeting with *Harper's* management: Morris 1993 (including quotations), p. 355.

72 "This has been an agonizing decision": Willie Morris Collection, WM to John Cowles Jr., 3/1/71.

73 "It all boiled down to the money men": Whitman.

73 Writers' reaction to Willie's resignation: *New York Times*, March 10, 1971.

73 "Acrimonious and complex": *New York Times*, March 19, 1971.

73 "Had not properly taken the measure": Decter, p. 63.

73 "We should never have gotten married": interview with Celia Morris.

73 "Nothing lasted": Morris 1993, p. 243.

73 "Almost overnight": Morris 1993, p. 364.

SIX: SELF-EXILE ON LONG ISLAND: "MOLDING FROM THIS ANOTHER LIFE"

74 "Molding from this another life": Morris 1993, p. 366.

74 "You are the best editor": Willie Morris Collection, James Dickey to WM, 5/21/71.

74 Willie's first glimpse of the Hamptons: *James Jones: A Friendship*, pp. 163–65.

74–75 Willie's time at Muriel Oxenberg Murphy's house: emails from Edwin M. Yoder Jr.

74–75 "Headstrong, self-inflicted exile" and "In the snowy solitude": Morris 1993, pp. 365–66.

75   "People were calling every 10 minutes": Edwin M. Yoder Jr. as quoted in Shnayerson.

75   Willie's job offers: Willie Morris Collection; Morris 1993, pp. 364–65.

75   "Please, Willie" and "Have you gone into seclusion?": Willie Morris Collection, 3/24/71 and 4/5/71.

76   "Still owned a typewriter" and "I thought about newspaper work again": Morris 1993, pp. 364–66.

76   "I said to myself": Bales 2000, p.173.

76   "It succeeds": Wakefield.

76   "You somehow bring": Willie Morris Collection, 3/8/71.

77   "I hope you will remember": Willie Morris Collection, 1/22/68.

77   "It has marvelous things in it" and "SOME thoughts about the race situation": Willie Morris Collection, Nordstrom to Daves, 10/27/70.

77   "Beginning, a real middle": Willie Morris Collection, Daves to WM, 1/6/71.

77   "Drenched in crawdads": *Time*, Dec. 27, 1971, as quoted in Bales 2006, p. 209.

77–78 "I cried when I read": Willie Morris Collection, 11/10/71.

78   "Watching the filming": Morris 1993, pp. 369–70.

78   Description of house on Church Lane: email from David Rae Morris.

78   Description of Bobby Van's and "the watering hole": Harrison, p. 116.

79   "Writer's community" and "talk about writing": Bales 2000, p. 33.

79   Willie and David Rae's visits: interview with David Rae Morris.

79   "You never answer": Willie Morris Collection, 10/5/71.

80   Letters from Celia Morris concerning alimony and child support: Willie Morris Collection, October–December 1971.

80   "That you had": Willie Morris Collection, 10/31/72.

80   "Drab and snowy": Morris 1994, Author's Note.

80   "The book sounds terrific": Willie Morris Collection, 1/27/72.

80   "I've promised myself": King 2006, p. 190.

81   "I know how painful it's been": Willie Morris Collection, 4/12/72.

81   "Drags along": letter to Sarah Cooper Lear Morrisette, 5/15/72; courtesy B. S. Ricks Memorial Library.

81   "About the greatest honor" and "the highest expression": Willie Morris Collection, 5/9/73.

81   Timing of Willie's relationship with Barbara Howar: emails from David Rae Morris.

81   "Great fun": Jonathan Yardley, "Yen for Power," *New Republic*, May 19, 1973, as quoted in Bales 2006, p. 210.

81   "Morris writes fine dialogue": Mano.

81–82 "Severely discombobulated," "kidnapped," and "through alimony": Morris 1994, Author's Note.

82 "She was 97": Morris 1981, p. 90.

82 "Grateful that you're doing": Willie Morris Collection, 12/12/74.

83 "A lightning bolt": Willie Morris Collection, 4/18/75.

83 "Perceptive and stirring": Gary Thatcher, "Deep South Paid Honor in Album," *Christian Science Monitor*, June 14, 1976, as quoted in Bales 2006, p. 214.

83 "Derivative drivel" and "foggy Faulkner": Hoagland.

83 "The piece attacked me" and "A serious writer must grow": *James Jones: A Friendship*, p. 210.

83 "My father just adored [Willie]": interview with Kaylie Jones.

83 "Often at night": *James Jones: A Friendship*, p. 176.

84 "At Chateau Spud": *James Jones: A Friendship*, p. 178.

84 Willie as Kaylie's godfather: interview with Kaylie Jones.

84 "Held together by Jeffersonian democracy": *James Jones: A Friendship*, p. 181.

85 "A village of dogs": *James Jones: A Friendship*, p. 186.

85 "Like some kind of modern-day Pied Piper": Kaylie Jones, p. 243.

85 "They were kindred spirits": interview with Kaylie Jones.

85–86 "I got a friend of mine": letter of 4/24/79; courtesy B. S. Ricks Memorial Library.

86 "Brilliant daily journalism": email from Edwin M. Yoder Jr.

87 "Willie is probably the finest line editor": Winston Groom's foreword to *James Jones: A Friendship*, p. viii.

87 "He read it and told me": Winston Groom, as quoted in King 2006, p. 214.

87 "Restless and nervous": Willie Morris Collection, letter from Ethel North, 12/25/76.

87 "Eat correctly": Willie Morris Collection, 2/15/77.

87 "The moment came": *James Jones: A Friendship*, p. 19.

88 "Two great presences": *James Jones: A Friendship*, p. 14.

88 "A sacred duty": interview with Kaylie Jones.

88 "One can scarcely tell": Aldridge.

88 "Something about writing": *James Jones: A Friendship*, p. ix.

88 "[It] is as much an autobiography": Lehmann-Haupt.

89 "Here is your copy": Willie Morris Collection, 11/21/78.

89 "The death of the last of one's parents": *James Jones: A Friendship*, p. 18.

89 "The only way this pain is assuaged": letter dated 9/2/78; courtesy B. S. Ricks Memorial Library.

SEVEN: "COMING BACK TO WHERE HIS STRONGEST FEELINGS LAY"

90 "Coming back to where his strongest feelings lay": Morris 1981, p. 8.

90 "Everything that matters in life": 8/24/84; courtesy Karen Hinton.

90   Willie's trip to Oxford, Mississippi, and arrival: interview with David Rae Morris; King 2006, p. 242.

90   "As if in a dream": Morris 1981, p. 8.

90   "It looks like I'm coming down": Bales 2000, p. 36.

91   Discussion about position for Willie at University of Mississippi: Willie Morris Collection, letters from Larry Wells to WM 10/9/78, 2/6/79, and 3/2/79; Farrar.

91   "Odd hesitations": Willie Morris Collection, letter to Jim Dees, 12/3/97.

91   University of Mississippi was recruiting African American students: Sansing, p. 324.

91   Description of Oxford and changes there: interview with Richard Howorth.

91   "Nerve ends": Bales 2000, pp. 51–52.

92   "I like the way they sell chicken": "The Ghosts of Ole Miss," *Inside Sports*, May 1980, reprinted in Morris 1981, p. 245.

92   "Willie liked to tell stories": interview with Richard Howorth.

93   "Graveyard talk": email from and interview with Ron Borne.

93   "Seventy-five of the best students": Morris 1989, p. 43.

94   Reading list for Willie's American literature course: Bales 2000, p. 117.

94   "He would put emphasis": interview with Karen Hinton.

95   "When you got past the top of the table": interview with Sid Salter.

95   "*Taps* was this haunting story": interview with Jim Dees.

95   Willie kept the *Taps* manuscript in his freezer: interview with Steve Yarbrough.

95   "I was only a kid": Willie Morris Collection, undated.

96   "Your Mississippi piece": Willie Morris Collection, 5/28/81.

96   David Halberstam's contribution to *The Courting of Marcus Dupree* and "It's a book right up your alley": Willie Morris Collection, 7/21/81.

96   "Devotion to Doubleday": Willie Morris Collection, 9/25/80.

96   Herman Gollob expressed interest in publishing Willie: Willie Morris Collection, letter to WM from Sterling Lord, 10/19/81.

97   "He was an incredible teacher": interview with Anne Glover.

97   "He knew a good story": interview with Will Norton.

97   "The potato field": Willie Morris Collection, 10/21/81 (illegible signature).

97   "As I said on the phone": letter of 5/18/82; courtesy David Rae Morris.

97   "I'm really getting concerned": Willie Morris Collection, 10/26/82.

97   "Something of me was gone with Pete": Morris 1992, p. 450.

98   "The story of a transformation": An edited version of the blurb appears on the paperback edition from the University Press of Mississippi.

99   "Affirm the highest values": The Christophers website (christophers.org).

99   "You have helped us recruit": Willie Morris Collection, 2/14/84.

99   "I've been writing magazine pieces": 8/24/84; courtesy Karen Hinton.

99   The university was supportive: Willie Morris Collection, letter from office of Robert Khayat to WM, 3/21/88.

100   JoAnne Prichard's ruse to meet Willie: interview with JoAnne Prichard Morris.

101   "Start hollering": Willie Morris Collection, 6/6/88.

101   "Why, as the feller said": Willie Morris Collection, 8/4/88.

101   "Without a doubt": Willie Morris Collection, 8/3/88.

101   "I know Herman": Willie Morris Collection, 8/11/88.

101   "I was so happy to get your letter": Willie Morris Collection, 10/10/88.

101   "I hope your work on *Taps* is productive": Willie Morris Collection, 12/27/88.

101–2   "We wanted a plot-driven novel": King 2006, p. 280.

102   Lord's other *Taps* submissions and Willie's decision to withdraw: Willie Morris Collection, letter from Sterling Lord, 8/2/89. Crown and Putnam rejected the manuscript; it was withdrawn from Houghton Mifflin.

102   Letter from David Rae: Willie Morris Collection, 5/8/89.

102   Willie's attitude toward drinking: interview with JoAnne Prichard Morris.

102–3   Willie's courtship of JoAnne and his proposal: interview with JoAnne Prichard Morris.

EIGHT: "BITTERSWEET, BUT FINE":
FINDING SERENITY IN JACKSON

105   "Bittersweet, but fine" and "At age 59, going on 60": Willie Morris Collection, 9/24/94.

105   Willie and JoAnne's wedding and reception: email from Cary Hill; interviews with JoAnne Prichard Morris and David Rae Morris.

106   "The most underrated motel": interview with JoAnne Prichard Morris.

106–7   "That this is a good place" and "He was the Pied Piper": interview with Malcolm White.

107–8   JoAnne and Willie's marriage and life in Jackson: interviews with JoAnne Prichard Morris and Ruth Williams.

107   "She was a Delta girl" and "lingering landscapes": Morris 1999, p. 21.

107   "She's the best editor": interview with Ruth Williams.

108–9   "Life was a lot more interesting," "Sometimes you have to lie," and "Willie liked to play": interview with JoAnne Prichard Morris.

109   "How about our taking bids": Willie Morris Collection, 3/3/91.

110   Celia thanked Willie and wished him well: Willie Morris Collection, letter from Celia Morris, undated.

110   "The Dungeon" and "did not exactly lock me in": Morris 1999, p. 68.

110   "I think only after we were married": interview with JoAnne Prichard Morris.

111   "An especially beautiful piece of writing": Brad Hooper, untitled review, *Booklist*, July 1993, as quoted in Bales 2006, p. 230.

111   "Purple prose": Florence King, "'Days' Rush by in a Blur of Words That Run You Over," *Washington Times*, August 29, 1993, as quoted in Bales 2006, p. 231.

111   "Vivid sequel" and "name-dropping": Wilda Williams, *Library Journal*, August 1993, as quoted in Bales 2006, p. 231.

III   "Occasionally oblique": Shaun O'Connell, "Falling from Gotham's Heights and Telling About It," *Boston Globe*, September 19, 1993, as quoted in Bales 2006, p. 234.

III   "Little good stuff": James Wolcott, "Remaking It," *New Republic*, November 15, 1993, p. 236, as quoted in Bales 2006, p. 236.

III   "More bemused than aggrieved": *New York Times Book Review*, December 19, 1993.

III   "I'm glad I waited": Bales 2000, p. 129.

112   "It gave him the chance": interview with David Rae Morris.

112   "I feel myself very much in the need": Willie Morris Collection, 12/1/93.

113   "I had been saying": interview with JoAnne Prichard Morris.

113   "An abundance of new material" and "top dollar": Willie Morris Collection, letter to Theron Raines, 7/94 (no day).

113   "I really felt wonderful": Willie Morris Collection, 8/11/94.

113   "This is the beginning": Willie Morris Collection, 8/25/94.

113   "I want this to be": Willie Morris Collection, 10/4/94.

114   "Absolutely loved the movies": interview with JoAnne Prichard Morris.

114   "'That's ol' Skip and me'": Willie Morris Collection, 11/29/94.

114–15 Description of Willie's sixtieth birthday party: interview with David Rae Morris.

114–15 "Malicious mischief" and other charges against Willie: Mock bench warrant signed by L. Breland Hilbury, Circuit Court Judge of Hinds County, Willie Morris Collection, 11/29/94.

115   "A continuing prodigious memory": Mock sentence signed by Judge E. Grady Jolly, Willie Morris Collection, 11/29/94.

116   "The Hollywood culture" and "racism in today's America": Willie Morris Collection, 8/14/96.

116   "Rather depressed": Willie Morris Collection, 3/18/98.

117   "You are keeping": Willie Morris Collection, 8/21/98.

117   "I'm going to write a book": interview with Jill Conner Browne.

117   "You just must remember": Willie Morris Collection, 3/28/94.

117   "Spit is wonderful": Willie Morris Collection, 1/7/99.

118   "Quite frankly I'm a little tired": Willie Morris Collection, 4/5/99.

118   Willie's first meeting with Eudora Welty and "She writes those stories": *Vanity Fair*, May 1999.

118   "Eudora, I'm going to make a left": *Vanity Fair*, May 1999; also letter from WM to Teresa Nicholas, 7/23/97.

118–19 Willie's Mother's Day note to JoAnne, 5/8/99: courtesy JoAnne Prichard Morris.

119   "A personal memoir about baseball" and "As I dwell on his story": letter to Robert Loomis, 7/12/99; courtesy JoAnne Prichard Morris.

120   Willie's last day, including quotations: interviews with JoAnne Prichard Morris, Fletcher and Carol Cox, David Rae Morris, Ruth Williams, John Langston, John Evans, and Jill Conner Browne.

121   "In a Mississippi of myths and legends": *Remembering Willie*, p. 26.

122 "Even across the divide of death": Morris 1981, p. 188, where the punctuation is slightly different: "Even across the divide of death, friendship remains, an echo forever in the heart."

EPILOGUE

123 "He showed us how we could love a place": Clinton.

123 "He could get someone else to paint his fence": interview with Malcolm White.

123 "Turn[ing] his childhood in Yazoo City": Applebome.

124 "Made pristine facts more actual than reality": *North Toward Home*, p. 112.

124 "A place belongs forever to whoever claims it hardest": Didion.

124 "Funny and endearing": Jonathan Yardley, "Small Tale: Learning to Love Cats," *Washington Post*, November 17, 1999, as quoted in Bales 2006, p. 245.

126 "Distinguished himself and Yazoo City": Sikes, Vernon, "City Officials Honor Morris with Resolution," *Yazoo Herald*, August 11, 1999, as quoted in Bales 2006, p. 358.

126 "When you write a book": Carr, p. 104.

126 Dedication of Willie Morris Library, including quotation: Minor.

126 "The numbness has worn off now": letter to Nadine Eckhardt, postmarked September 2, 1999; courtesy David Rae Morris.

126 "Putting the moon" and *Taps* publication plans: Rosen.

126 "Although I had some hesitation": Morris 2001, p. 339.

127 "I have a vivid recurring dream": Morris 2001, pp. 337–38.

Bibliography

WORKS BY WILLIE MORRIS
Books

(Only books cited in the text are listed here; for a complete list of his works, see "Books by Willie Morris," p. 133.)

The Courting of Marcus Dupree. Jackson: University Press of Mississippi, 1992. Originally published in 1983 by Doubleday & Company.

Homecomings. Jackson: University Press of Mississippi, 1989. With the art of William Dunlap.

James Jones: A Friendship. Urbana: University of Illinois Press, 2000. Originally published in 1978 by Doubleday & Company.

The Last of the Southern Girls. Baton Rouge: Louisiana State University Press, 1994. Originally published in 1973 by Alfred A. Knopf, Inc.

My Cat Spit McGee. New York: Random House, 1999.

My Dog Skip. New York: Random House, 1995.

My Two Oxfords. Jackson: University Press of Mississippi, 2009. Originally published in 1992 by Yellow Barn Press.

New York Days. Boston: Little, Brown and Company, 1993.

North Toward Home. New York: Vintage Books, 2000. Originally published in 1967 by Houghton Mifflin Company.

Shifting Interludes. Edited by Jack Bales. Jackson: University Press of Mississippi, 2002.

Taps. Boston: Houghton Mifflin Company, 2001.

Terrains of the Heart and Other Essays on Home. Oxford, Mississippi: Yoknapatawpha Press, 1981.

Unpublished childhood diary; courtesy JoAnne Prichard Morris.

Articles

(Arranged by date)

"Can We Carry Out That Faith?," *Flashlight*, May 29, 1952.

"Well, Here I Am," *Daily Texan*, September 17, 1952.

"Neighboring News," *Daily Texan*, September 18, 1952.

"Campus Sidelights: Brackenridge 'Refugees' Not Thirsty These Days," *Daily Texan*, April 1, 1953.

"Assignment Forty Acres," *Daily Texan*, April 8, 1953.

"The Round-Up," *Daily Texan*, February 11, 1954.

"The Round-Up," *Daily Texan*, May 14, 1954.

"Bevo Will Trek to ND to Spoil the Irish Jig," *Daily Texan*, September 21, 1954.

"Bevo Is Sensation on Midwest Jaunt," *Daily Texan*, September 24, 1954.

"The Round-Up," *Daily Texan*, September 29, 1954.

"The Round-Up," *Daily Texan*, October 20, 1954.

"Best Solution Must Be Slow," *Daily Texan*, December 5, 1954.

"A New Year for the Texan—We'll Play Hard and Clean," *Daily Texan*, June 7, 1955.

"The Round-Up," *Daily Texan*, June 7, 1955.

"Looking Backward: Have We Reneged?" *Daily Texan*, November 11, 1955.

"Don't Walk on Grass," *Daily Texan*, February 8, 1956.

"Let's Water the Pansies," *Daily Texan*, February 9, 1956.

"Prerogative of Dissent Defended by Texan," February 9, 1956.

"This Editorial Withheld," *Daily Texan*, February 28, 1956.

"Outgoing, Incoming Editors Talk" (with Ronnie Dugger), *Texas Observer*, December 16, 1960.

"Foreword," *Harper's*, April 1965.

"From Willie to Bo, Others," *Yazoo City Herald*, October 19, 1967.

Letter to the editor, *New York Times Book Review*, December 19, 1993.

"Mississippi Queen," *Vanity Fair*, May 1999.

OTHER SOURCES

Aldridge, John W. "The Last James Jones," *New York Times*, March 5, 1978.

Applebome, Peter. "Willie Morris, 64, Writer on the Southern Experience," *New York Times*, August 3, 1999.

Bales, Jack. *Willie Morris: An Exhaustive Annotated Bibliography and a Biography*. Jefferson, North Carolina: McFarland & Company, 2006.

———, ed. *Conversations with Willie Morris*. Jackson: University Press of Mississippi, 2000.

Cactus (University of Texas yearbook), 1953–56.

Carr, John. *Kite-Flying and Other Irrational Acts: Conversations with Twelve Southern Writers*. Baton Rouge: Louisiana State University Press, 1972.

Clinton, Bill. "Eulogy: Willie Morris." *Time*, August 16, 1999.

Collins, Clifton (Bo), Jr. "'Bo' Collins to Willie," *Yazoo City Herald*, October 12, 1967.

Copp, Tara, and Robert L. Rogers. *The Daily Texan: The First 100 Years*. Austin: Eakin Press, 1999.

Corry, John. *My Times: Adventures in the News Trade*. New York: G. P. Putnam's Sons, 1993.

Couch, Sandra. "Sweetheart's a Champ; Wins Grades, Contests," *Daily Texan*, April 8, 1956.

Daily Texan. "Texan Editor," April 27, 1955.

———. "UT Voters Put Farabee, Morris, Siegel, Holder, Richards In; Yell Leader Run-off," April 27, 1955.

————. "Friars Select Four New Members," November 6, 1955.

————. "Regents' Statement," February 8, 1956.

————. "Dobie Blasts Regents," February 9, 1956.

————. "Charmin' Celia Cradles Campus Crown," April 8, 1956.

DeCell, Harriet, and JoAnne Prichard. *Yazoo: Its Legends and Legacies.* Yazoo City, Mississippi: Yazoo Delta Press, 1976.

Decter, Midge. *An Old Wife's Tale: My Seven Decades in Love and War.* New York: ReganBooks, 2001.

Didion, Joan. *The White Album.* New York: Farrar, Straus and Giroux, 1990. Originally published in 1979 by Simon & Schuster.

Dobie, J. Frank. "Dobie Blasts Regents," *Daily Texan,* February 9, 1956.

Dugger, Ronnie. "Death of the Texan," *Daily Texan,* April 17, 1956.

————. "Outgoing, Incoming Editors Talk" (with WM), *Texas Observer,* December 16, 1960.

Eckhardt, Nadine. *Duchess of Palms: A Memoir.* Austin: University of Texas Press, 2009.

Farrar, Ronald. *Powerhouse: The Meek School at Ole Miss.* Oxford: Yoknapatawpha Press, 2014.

Fischer, John. "The Editor's Easy Chair," *Harper's,* July 1967.

Flashlight (Yazoo City High School newspaper). "55 Senior Graduates Receive Sheepskins," May 29, 1952.

————. "'Flashlight' Cops National Awards in Press Contests," May 29, 1952.

————. "Party-Poopers Play Paltry Parts; Pickled 'til June," May 29, 1952.

————. "Seniors Tell Their Future; Majority Will Attend School," May 29, 1952.

Grantham, Margaret Pepper. *Darkness on the Delta,* 2002 (film).

Hardy, Thomas. *Jude the Obscure.* Mineola, New York: Dover Publications, 2006. Originally published in 1895.

Harrison, Helen A., and Constance Ayers Denne. *Hamptons Bohemia: Two Centuries of Artists and Writers on the Beach.* San Francisco: Chronicle Books, 2002.

Hoagland, Edward. "Down Memory Lane," *New York Times Book Review,* December 7, 1975.

Johnson, Ellen. "Family, Music, Antiques—Marion's Loves," *Yazoo City Herald,* March 9, 1972.

Jones, Kaylie. *Lies My Mother Never Told Me: A Memoir.* New York: Harper Perennial, 2010.

Jones, Madison. "Journey from Yazoo," *New York Times Book Review,* October 22, 1967.

Kihss, Peter. "50% of Harper's Magazine Sold to Cowles Paper in Minneapolis," *New York Times,* April 29, 1965.

King, Larry L. *In Search of Willie Morris: The Mercurial Life of a Legendary Writer and Editor.* New York: PublicAffairs, 2006.

————. *None But a Blockhead: On Being a Writer.* New York: Penguin Books, 1987.

————. *A Writer's Life in Letters, Or, Reflections in a Bloodshot Eye.* Fort Worth: TCU Press, 1999.

Lehmann-Haupt, Christopher. "Books of the Times," *New York Times,* November 15, 1978.

Mano, D. Keith. Untitled review, *New York Times Book Review*, May 20, 1973.

McDowell, Edwin. "For Publishing, the City Remains 'the Mecca,'" *New York Times*, March 15, 1983.

Mingo Chito (Yazoo City High School yearbook), 1949, 1951, 1952.

Minor, Bill. "Library Honors Willie Morris," *Clarksdale Press Register*, December 8, 2006.

Morris, Celia. *Finding Celia's Place*. College Station: Texas A&M University Press, 2000.

New York Times. "$2,000,000 Fire in Yazoo City," May 26, 1904.

———. "3 Pulitzer Winners Make Harper's Plea," March 10, 1971.

———. "Harper's to Select a New Editor Soon," March 19, 1971.

O'Beirne, Frank. *The Harpers of Virginia, West Virginia, and Mississippi*. Unpublished manuscript, 1982. Courtesy David Rae Morris.

Remembering Willie (no author credit). Jackson: University Press of Mississippi, 2000.

Rosen, Judith. "'Taps' for Willie Morris," *Publishers Weekly*, April 2, 2001.

Sansing, David. *The University of Mississippi: A Sesquicentennial History*. Jackson: University Press of Mississippi, 1999.

Shnayerson, Michael. "He'll Always Have Elaine's," *Vanity Fair*, October 1993.

Styron, Rose, ed., with R. Blakeslee Gilpin. *Selected Letters of William Styron*. New York: Random House, 2012.

Wakefield, Dan. Untitled review, *New York Times*, May 16, 1971.

Whitman, Alden. "Morris Resigns in Harper's Dispute," *New York Times*, March 5, 1971.

Yazoo City Herald. "'Non-Discriminatory Basis' NAACP Asks School Board," August 18, 1955.

———. "Public Invited to Meeting of Citizens Council Friday," August 25, 1955.

———. "Only 6 Names Left on List; Lions to Hear 'Tut' Patterson," September 1, 1955.

———. Society page, August 21, 1958.

———. Obituary of Rae Morris, September 4, 1958.

Yazoo Sentinel, September 23, 1916.

Yoder, Edwin M., Jr. *Telling Others What to Think: Recollections of a Pundit*. Baton Rouge: Louisiana State University Press, 2004.

Photo Credits

Photographs on pages vi and 58 by Burton Berinsky.

Photographs on the following pages are courtesy of Archives and Special Collections, University of Mississippi Libraries: 7, 9, 10, 12, 13, 15, 16, 25, 46, 58, 63, 80, 89, and 106. The photograph of Marion Morris on page 7 was taken by Stanley Beers.

Photographs on pages 4 and 8 are courtesy of the Morris family.

The photograph on page 27 was taken by Stanley Beers and is courtesy of B. S. Ricks Memorial Library.

Photographs on the following pages are courtesy of JoAnne Prichard Morris: 19, 20, and 49. The photograph on page 20 was taken by Dane Hemenway.

The photograph on page 26 is from a December 1949 issue of the *Flashlight*, courtesy of JoAnne Prichard Morris.

Photographs on pages 23, 24, and 28 are from the 1952 edition of the *Mingo Chito*, courtesy of Margaret Pepper Grantham.

Photographs on pages 31, 32, 36, and 38 are published by permission of the *Cactus* at the University of Texas–Austin.

Photographs on pages 30 and 39 are published by permission of the *Daily Texan* at the University of Texas–Austin.

Photographs on pages 43 and 51 are courtesy of Celia Morris.

Photograph on page 47 by Pete Spiro/Shutterstock.

The photograph on page 52 © 2015 Alan Pogue.

The photograph of the Texas state capitol on page 54 © 2015 Teresa Nicholas.

The photograph of Scholz Garten on page 54 is courtesy of Tom Davis, Scholz Garten.

The photograph on page 66 is courtesy of Norman A. Mott Jr.

The photograph on page 69 was created by Delk, UT Texas Student Publications, Prints and Photographs Collection, di_09888, the Dolph Briscoe Center for American History, University of Texas at Austin.

The photograph on page 72 © 1971 The Associated Press.

Photographs on pages 78, 79, 84, 85, 86, 93, 94, 98, 100, 112, 115, and 125 © David Rae Morris.

The photograph on page 89 is courtesy of Lou Schwartz.

Photographs on pages 102 and 103 are published by permission of William Ferris, the Southern Folklife Collection, Louis Round Wilson Special Collections Library, University of North Carolina at Chapel Hill.

The photograph on page 106 is courtesy of William H. Morris Jr.

Photographs on pages 107 and 109 are courtesy of Hunter Cole.

The photograph on page 121 is courtesy of the *Clarion-Ledger*.

Index

Page numbers in **bold** indicate illustrations.